W9-DCH-930

INSIDER'S GUIDE TO TEACHING WITH

COLLEGE ALGEBRA: GRAPHS & MODELS
FOURTH EDITION

Marvin L. Bittinger
Indiana University Purdue University Indianapolis

Judith A. Beecher
Indiana University Purdue University Indianapolis

David J. Ellenbogen
Community College of Vermont

Judith A. Penna
Indiana University Purdue University Indianapolis

PEARSON
Addison
Wesley

Boston San Francisco New York
London Toronto Sydney Tokyo Singapore Madrid
Mexico City Munich Paris Cape Town Hong Kong Montreal

Publisher	Greg Tobin
Executive Editor	Anne Kelly
Senior Managing Editor	Karen Wernholm
Senior Project Editor	Rachel S. Reeve
Developmental Editor	Sharon Testone
Assistant Editors	Leah Goldberg
Production Supervisor	Kathleen Manley
Production Coordinator	Kayla Smith-Tarbox
Digital Assets Manager	Marianne Groth
Manufacturing Manager	Evelyn Beaton
Composition	Suzanne Roark
Executive Marketing Manager	Becky Anderson
Marketing Coordinator	Bonnie Gill

⚠ **This work is protected by United States copyright laws and is provided solely for the use of instructors in teaching their courses and assessing student learning. Dissemination or sale of any part of this work (including on the World Wide Web) will destroy the integrity of the work and is not permitted. The work and materials from it should never be made available to students except by instructors using the accompanying text in their classes. All recipients of this work are expected to abide by these restrictions and to honor the intended pedagogical purposes and the needs of other instructors who rely on these materials.**

Reproduced by Pearson Addison-Wesley from electronic files supplied by the author.

Copyright © 2009 Pearson Education, Inc.
Publishing as Pearson Addison-Wesley, 75 Arlington Street, Boston, MA 02116.

All rights reserved. No part of this publication may be reproduced, stored in a retrieval system, or transmitted, in any form or by any means, electronic, mechanical, photocopying, recording, or otherwise, without the prior written permission of the publisher. Printed in the United States of America.

ISBN-13: 978-0-321-52912-1
ISBN-10: 0-321-52912-X

1 2 3 4 5 6 OPM 11 10 09 08

CONTENTS

Introduction iv

Getting Started 1

General Teaching Advice 9

Sample Syllabus 13

Teaching Tips Correlated to Textbook Sections 17

Available Supplements 53

MathXL Overview 55

MyMathLab Overview 56

Helpful Tips for Using Supplements and Technology 57

Conversion Guide from the Third Edition to the Fourth Edition 59

Useful Classroom Resources for Teachers 61

Transparency Masters and Test Aids 65

Professional Bibliography 75

INTRODUCTION

Dear Faculty:

The Bittinger, Beecher, Ellenbogen, and Penna book team at Pearson Addison-Wesley is very excited that you will be using *College Algebra: Graphs & Models*, Fourth Edition. We know that whether you are teaching this course for the first time or the tenth time, you will face many challenges, including how to prepare for class, how to make the most effective use of your class time, how to present the material to your students in a manner that will make sense to them, how to access your students, what resources are available, and what other teachers have done in the past.

This manual is designed to make your job easier. Inside these pages are words of advice from experienced instructors, general and content-specific teaching tips, tips on using both student and instructor supplements that accompany this text, and a professional bibliography provided by your fellow instructors. Insider's Guides are also available for the remaining titles in the series: *Algebra and Trigonometry: Graphs & Models*, Fourth Edition and *Precalculus: Graphs & Models*, Fourth Edition.

We would like to thank the following professors for sharing their advice and teaching tips. This manual would not have been possible without their valuable contributions.

Marc D. Campbell, *Daytona Beach Community College*

Tim Chappell, *Penn Valley Community College*

Amy Del Medico, *Waubonsee Community College*

Luke Dowell, *Seward County Community College*

Nicki Feldman, *Pulaski Technical College*

Bridgette L. Jacob, *Onondaga Community College*

Renée M. Macaluso, *Arizona Western College*

Caroline Martinson, *Jefferson Community College*

Pavel Sikorskii, *Michigan State University*

It is also important to know that you have a very valuable resource available to you in your Pearson sales representative. It you do not know your representative, you can locate him/her by logging on to www.aw-bc.com/replocator and typing in the zip code of your institution. Please feel free to contact your representative if you have any questions relating to our text of if you need additional supplements. Of course, you can always contact us directly at math@aw.com.

We know that teaching this course can be challenging. We hope that this and the other resources we have provided will help to minimize the amount of time it takes you to meet those challenges.

Good luck in your endeavors!

The Bittinger, Beecher, Ellenbogen, and Penna book team

GETTING STARTED

1. **How to Be an Effective Teacher**   3
   Five principles of good teaching practice

   Tips for Thriving: Creating an Inclusive Classroom

2. **Planning Your Course**   4
   Constructing the syllabus
   Problems to avoid

   Tips for Thriving: Visual Quality

3. **Your First Class**   4
   Seven goals for a successful first meeting

4. **Strategies for Teaching and Learning**   5
   Team learning

   Tips for Thriving: Active Learning and Lecturing

5. **Grading and Assessment Techniques**   6
   Philosophy of grading
   Criterion grading

   Tips for Thriving: Result Feedback

6. **Managing Problem Situations**   7
   Cheating
   Unmotivated students

   Tips for Thriving: Discipline

   Credibility problems

7. **Improving Your Performance**   8
   Self-evaluation

   Tips for Thriving: Video-Recording Your Class

References   8

1   How to Be an Effective Teacher

(From David Royse, *Teaching Tips for College and University Instructors: A Practical Guide*, published by Allyn & Bacon, Boston, MA. © 2001 by Pearson Education, Inc. Adapted by permission of the publisher.)

A look at 50 years of research "on the way teachers teach and learners learn" reveals five broad principles of good teaching practice (Chickering and Gamson, 1987).

Five Principles of Good Teaching Practice

1. **Frequent student-faculty contact:** Faculty who are concerned about their students and their progress and who are perceived to be easy to talk to serve to motivate and keep students involved.

   Things you can do to apply this principle:
   - Attend events sponsored by students.
   - Serve as a mentor or advisor to students.
   - Keep "open" or "drop-in" office hours.

2. **The encouragement of cooperation among students:** There is a wealth of research indicating that students benefit from the use of small-group and peer-learning instructional approaches.

   Things you can do to apply this principle:
   - Have students share in class their interests and backgrounds.
   - Create small groups to work on projects together.
   - Encourage students to study together.

3. **Prompt feedback:** Learning theory research has consistently shown that the quicker the feedback, the greater the learning.

   Things you can do to apply this principle:
   - Return quizzes and exams by the next class meeting.
   - Return homework within one week.
   - Provide students with detailed comments on their written papers.

4. **Emphasize time on task:** This principle refers to the amount of actual involvement with the material being studied and applies, obviously, to the way the instructor uses classroom instructional time. Faculty need good time-management skills.

   Things you can do to apply this principle:
   - Require students who miss classes to make up lost work.
   - Require students to rehearse before making oral presentations.
   - Don't let class breaks stretch out too long.

5. **Communicating high expectations:** The key here is not to make the course impossibly difficult but to have goals that can be attained as long as individual learners stretch and work hard, going beyond what they already know.

   Things you can do to apply this principle:
   - Communicate your expectations orally and in writing at the beginning of the course.
   - Explain the penalties for students who turn work in late.
   - Identify excellent work by students; display exemplars if possible.

✔ Tips for Thriving:

Creating an Inclusive Classroom

How do you model an open, accepting attitude within your classroom where students will feel it is safe to engage in give-and-take discussions? First, view students as individuals instead of representatives of separate and distinct groups. Cultivate a climate that is respectful of diverse viewpoints, and don't allow ridicule or defamatory and hurtful remarks. Try to encourage everyone in the class to participate and be alert to showing favoritism.

2   Planning Your Course

(From David Royse, *Teaching Tips for College and University Instructors: A Practical Guide*, published by Allyn & Bacon, Boston, MA. © 2001 by Pearson Education, Inc. Adapted by permission of the publisher.)

Constructing the syllabus: The syllabus should clearly communicate course objectives, assignments, required readings, and grading policies. Think of the syllabus as a stand-alone document. Those students who miss the first or second meeting of a class should be able to learn most of what they need to know about the requirements of the course from reading the syllabus. Start by collecting syllabi from colleagues who have recently taught the course you will be teaching and look for common threads and themes.

Problems to avoid: One mistake commonly made by educators teaching a course for the first time is that they may have rich and intricate visions of how they want students to demonstrate comprehension and synthesis of the material, but they somehow fail to convey this information to those enrolled. Check your syllabus to make sure your expectations have been fully articulated. Be very specific. Avoid vaguely worded instructions that can be misinterpreted.

✔ Tips for Thriving:

Visual Quality

Students today are highly visual learners, so you should give special emphasis to the visual quality of the materials you provide to students. Incorporate graphics into your syllabus and other handouts. Color-code your materials so material for different sections of the course are on different colored papers. Such visuals are likely to create a perception among students that you are contemporary.

3   Your First Class

(From Richard E. Lyons, Marcella L. Kysilka, & George E. Pawlas, *The Adjunct Professor's Guide to Success: Surviving and Thriving In The Classroom*, published by Allyn & Bacon, Boston, MA. © 1999 by Pearson Education, Inc. Adapted by permission of the publisher.)

Success in achieving a great start is almost always directly attributable to the quality and quantity of planning that has been invested by the course professor. If the first meeting of your class is to be successful, you should strive to achieve seven distinct goals.

Seven Goals for a Successful First Meeting

1. **Create a positive first impression:** Renowned communications consultant Roger Ailes claims you have fewer than 10 seconds to create a positive image of yourself. Students are greatly influenced by the visual component; therefore, you must look the part of the professional professor. Dress as you would for a professional job interview. Greet each student entering the room. Be approachable and genuine.

2. **Introduce yourself effectively:** Communicate to students who you are and why you are credible as the teacher of the course. Seek to establish your approachability by "building common ground," such as stating your understanding of students' hectic lifestyles or their common preconceptions toward the subject matter.

3. **Clarify the goals and expectations:** Make a transparency of each page of the syllabus for display on an overhead projector and, using a cover sheet, expose each section as you explain it. Provide clarification and elicit questions.

4. **Conduct an activity that introduces students to each other:** Students' chances of being able to complete a course effectively are enhanced if each comes to perceive classmates as a support network. The small amount of time you invest in an icebreaker will help create a positive classroom atmosphere and pay additional dividends throughout the term.

5. **Learn students' names:** A student who is regularly addressed by name feels more valued, is invested more effectively in classroom discussion, and will approach the professor with questions and concerns.

6. **Whet students' appetites for the course material:** The textbook adopted for the course is critical to your success. Your first meeting should include a review of its approach, features, and sequencing. Explain to students what percentage of class tests will be derived from material from the textbook.

7. **Reassure students of the value of the course:** At the close of your first meeting reassure students that the course will be a valuable learning experience and a wise investment of their time. Review the reasons why the course is a good investment: important and relevant content, interesting classmates, and a dynamic classroom environment.

4 Strategies for Teaching and Learning

(From David Royse, *Teaching Tips for College and University Instructors: A Practical Guide*, published by Allyn & Bacon, Boston, MA. © 2001 by Pearson Education, Inc. Adapted by permission of the publisher.)

Team learning: The essential features of this small-group learning approach, developed originally for use in large college classrooms are (1) relatively permanent heterogeneous task groups; (2) grading based on a combination of individual performance, group performance, and peer evaluation; (3) organization of the course so that the majority of class time is spent on small-group activities; (4) a six-step instructional process similar to the following model:

1. Individual study of material outside of the class is assigned.
2. Individual testing is used (multiple-choice questions over homework at the beginning of class).
3. Groups discuss their answers and then are given a group test of the same items. They then get immediate feedback (answers).
4. Groups may prepare written appeals of items.
5. Feedback is given from instructor.
6. An application-oriented activity is assigned (e.g., a problem to be solved requiring input from all group members).

If you plan to use team learning in your class, inform students at the beginning of the course of your intentions to do so and explain the benefits of small-group learning. Foster group cohesion by sitting groups together and letting them choose "identities" such as a team name or slogan. You will need to structure and supervise the groups and ensure that the projects build on newly acquired learning. Make the projects realistic and interesting and ensure that they are adequately structured so that each member contributes equally. Students should be given criteria by which they can assess and evaluate the contributions of their peers on a project-by-project basis (Michaelson, 1994).

✔ Tips for Thriving:

Active Learning and Lecturing

Lecturing is one of the most time-honored teaching methods, but does it have a place in an active learning environment? There are times when lecturing can be effective. Think about the following when planning a lecture:

Build interest: Capture your students' attention by leading off with an anecdote or cartoon.
Maximize understanding and retention: Use brief handouts and demonstrations as a visual backup to enable your students to see as well as hear.
Involve students during the lecture: Interrupt the lecture occasionally to challenge students to answer spot quiz questions.
Reinforce the lecture: Give students a self-scoring review test at the end of the lecture.

5   Grading and Assessment Techniques

(From Philip C. Wankat, *The Effective, Efficient Professor: Teaching, Scholarship And Service*, published by Allyn & Bacon, Boston, M. © 2002 by Pearson Education, Inc. Adapted by permission of the publisher.)

Philosophy of grading: Develop your own philosophy of grading by picturing in your mind the performance of typical A students, B students, and so on. Try different grading methods until you find one that fits your philosophy and is reasonably fair. Always look closely at students on grade borders—take into account personal factors if the group is small. Be consistent with or slightly more generous than the procedure outlined in your syllabus.

Criterion grading: Professor Philip Wankat writes: "I currently use a form of criterion grading for my sophomore and junior courses. I list the scores in the syllabus that will guarantee the students A's, B's, and so forth. For example, a score of 85 to 100 guarantees an A; 75 to 85, a B; 65 to 75, a C; and 55 to 65, a D. If half the class gets above 85%, they all get an A. This reduces competition and allows students to work together and help each other. The standard grade gives students something to aim for and tells them exactly what their grade is at any time. For students whose net scores are close to the borders at the end of the course, I look at other factors such as attendance before deciding a final grade."

✔ Tips for Thriving:

Result Feedback

As stated earlier, feedback on results is the most effective of motivating factors. Anxious students are especially hungry for positive feedback. You can quickly and easily provide it by simply writing "Great job!" on answer sheets or tests. For students who didn't perform well, a brief note such as "I'd love to talk with you at the end of class" can be especially reassuring. The key is to be proactive and maintain high standards while requiring students to retain ownership of their success.

(From Philip C. Wankat, *The Effective, Efficient Professor: Teaching, Scholarship And Service,* published by Allyn & Bacon, Boston, MA. © 2002 by Pearson Education, Inc. Adapted by permission of the publisher.)

Cheating: Cheating is one behavior that should not be tolerated. Tolerating cheating tends to make it worse. Prevention of cheating is much more effective than trying to cure it once it has occurred. A professor can prevent cheating by:

- Creating rapport with students.
- Gaining a reputation for giving fair tests.
- Giving clear instructions and guidelines before, during, and after tests.
- Educating students on the ethics of plagiarism.
- Requiring periodic progress reports and outlines before a paper is due.

Try to develop exams that are perceived as fair and secure by students. Often, the accusation that certain questions were tricky is valid as it relates to ambiguous language and trivial material. Ask your mentor or an experienced instructor to closely review the final draft of your first few exams for these factors.

(From David Royse, *Teaching Tips for College and University Instructors: A Practical Guide,* published by Allyn & Bacon, Boston, MA. © 2001 by Pearson Education, Inc. Adapted by permission of the publisher.)

Unmotivated students: There are numerous reasons why students may not be motivated. The "required course" scenario is a likely explanation—although politics in colonial America is your life's work, it is safe to assume that not everyone will share your enthusiasm. Lack of motivation can sometimes be attributed to personal reasons such as death of a loved one or depression. Whenever you detect a pattern that you assume to be due to lack of motivation (e.g., missing classes, not handing assignments in on time, nonparticipation in class), arrange a time to have the student meet with you outside the classroom. Candidly express your concerns and then listen.

Motivating students is part of faculty members' jobs. To increase motivation, professors should show enthusiasm for the topic, use various media and methods to present material, use humor in the classroom, employ activities that encourage active learning, and give frequent, positive feedback.

✔ Tips for Thriving:

Discipline

One effective method for dealing with some discipline problems is to ask the class for feedback (Angelo & Cross, 1993). In a one-minute quiz, ask the students, "What can I do to help you learn?" Collate the responses and present them to the class. If behavior such as excessive talking appears in some responses (e.g., "Tell people to shut up"), this gives you the backing to ask students to be quiet. Use of properly channeled peer pressure is often effective in controlling undesired behavior.

(From Sharon Baiocco, Jamie N. De Waters, *Successful College Teaching: Problem Solving Strategies of Distinguished Professors,* published by Allyn & Bacon, Boston, MA. © 1998 by Pearson Education, Inc. Adapted by permission of the publisher.)

Credibility problems: If you are an inexperienced instructor, you may have problems with students not taking you seriously. At the first class meeting, articulate clear rules of classroom decorum and conduct yourself with dignity and respect for students. Try to exude that you are in charge and are the "authority" and avoid trying to pose as the students' friend.

(From Richard E. Lyons, Marcella L. Kysilka & George E. Pawlas, *The Adjunct Professor's Guide to Success: Surviving and Thriving In The Classroom,* published by Allyn & Bacon, Boston, MA. © 1999 by Pearson Education, Inc. Adapted by permission of the publisher.)

Self-evaluation: The instructor who regularly engages in systematic self-evaluation will unquestionably derive greater reward from the formal methods of evaluation commonly employed by colleges and universities. One method for providing structure to an ongoing system of self-evaluation is to keep a journal of reflections on your teaching experiences. Regularly invest 15 or 20 introspective minutes following each class meeting to focus especially on the strategies and events in class that you feel could be improved or worked well. Committing your thoughts and emotions enables you to develop more effective habits, build confidence in your teaching performance, and make more effective comparisons later. The following questions will help guide self-assessment:

How do I typically begin a class?
Where/How do I position myself in the class?
How do I move in the classroom?
Where are my eyes usually focused?
Do I facilitate students' visual processing of course material?
Do I change the speed, volume, energy, and tone of my voice?
How do I ask questions of students?
How often, and when, do I smile or laugh in class?
How do I react when students are inattentive?
How do I react when students disagree with or challenge what I say?
How do I typically end a class?

✔ Tips for Thriving:

Video-Recording Your Class

In recent years, many professionals have markedly improved their job performance by employing video recorders in their preparation efforts. As an instructor, an effective method might be to ask your mentor or another colleague to tape a 10- to 15-minute mini-lesson, then to debrief it using the assessment questions above. Critiquing a videotaped session provides objectivity and is therefore more likely to effect change. Involving a colleague as an informal coach will enable you to gain from his/her experience and perspective and will reduce the chances of your engaging in self-deprecation.

References

Ailes, R. (1996). *You are the message: Getting what you want by being who you are.* New York: Doubleday.

Chickering, A. W., & Gamson, Z. F. (1987). "Seven principles for good practice in undergraduate education." *AAHE Bulletin* 39, 3–7.

Michaelson, L. K. (1994). Team Learning: Making a case for the small-group option. In K. W. Prichard & R. M. Sawyer (eds.), *Handbook of college teaching.* Westport, CT: Greenwood Press.

Sorcinelli, M. D. (1991). Research findings on the seven principles. In A.W. Chickering & Z. Gamson (eds.), "Applying the seven principles of good practice in undergraduate education." *New Directions for Teaching and Learning* 47. San Francisco: Jossey-Bass.

GENERAL TEACHING ADVICE

We asked the contributing professors for words of advice to instructors who are teaching this course. Their responses can be found on the following pages.

Marc D. Campbell, *Daytona Beach Community College*

1. Get organized. Organize your personal papers and classroom materials before you get to class.
2. Introduce yourself. Share an autobiographical sketch with your students.
3. Establish clear expectations. Immediately convey the expectations you have of your students and what they can expect from you as their instructor.
4. Make a good impression. The first impression is a lasting impression. Let your students know you are there for them and you want them to be successful.
5. Learn their names. Learn your students' names as soon as you can.
6. Foster a positive class atmosphere. Create an atmosphere that encourages. In some cases, reward students for speaking up in class, either to ask or answer a question.
7. Find a shoulder to lean on. If you don't have a colleague who's a "buddy," find one.
8. Get students involved. Identify ways you can include student participation in your lecture through group work, board work, and so on.
9. Be positive! Find opportunities to give positive feedback to your students.
10. Build spirit. Find something unique about your class — something you and your students can be proud about — and encourage it.
11. Keep good records. Get advice from your colleagues to help find a system that works.
12. Build student relationships. Encourage your students to work in groups, share telephone numbers, and/or let them work in pairs during class. Encourage them to get to know their classmates.
13. Promote your image. You are the best PR there is for education.
14. Be fair. Respect your students, and manage your classroom in an even-handed manner.
15. Relax! Remember that you are only one person, and you are doing the best you can.
16. Keep a sense of humor!

Tim Chappell, *Penn Valley Community College*

1. Talk to several veteran teachers who are teaching this course. By talking to several different teachers, you can find commonality in your discussions as well as unique teaching approaches. Ask pointed questions, such as:
   a. What sections are usually covered in the class? Are all these sections mandatory or are some optional?
   b. What sections (or topics) are most important in the course?
   c. What, if any, sections (or topics) can be covered lightly or omitted if time becomes an issue?
   d. Is there a departmental policy regarding technology?
2. Develop an atmosphere for learning. Get to know your students. Take roll the first day of class, making sure to get the correct pronunciation of each student's given name or the name the student prefers to go by. Tell the students about yourself and what prompted you to like mathematics as well as to teach mathematics. Discuss your philosophy of teaching, your teaching style, and how typical class sessions are structured.
3. Expect students to have some "holes" in their understanding of prerequisite material. As you cover topics that build on prerequisite material, provide a brief review of that material. Explain to students that if the review is not sufficient, then they need to bring themselves up to speed with that material.

4. Read the textbook. Make notes of where the author uses a different approach than you do and tell the students when you lecture on those topics.

5. Make sure that your lecture or group work prepares the students for the homework you assign. Make sure the homework you assign prepares the students for the tests you give. I limit my questions to 15 questions for a 50–55 minute class session. I also give my students a concept review sheet that lists all the concepts covered in that unit. I make it clear to the students that I use the concept review sheet as a guide when I make up the test. If they want to know what is on the test, they should study the concept review sheet. I have a sample test online as well, but I caution students to use it as an example of the length and type of test I give, not as a carbon copy of the actual test. I also make it a priority to grade the tests and return them by the next class session.

Amy Del Medico, *Waubonsee Community College*

1. Always be prepared. Try to anticipate students' questions and difficulties. By having examples or explanations ready to go, you can easily and quickly answer their questions.

2. Grade and return papers as quickly as possible. Every time I take longer than promised to return a set of papers, a comment about it shows up on my teaching evaluations. This is clearly very important to students, and I think even more so in math courses.

3. Wait longer than you feel is comfortable after asking "Are there any questions?" It can take a good 5 – 10 seconds for students to formulate their questions before they ask them. So only waiting 3 seconds is not enough time. Time yourself to see how long 10 seconds of being silent really takes and how it feels.

4. Write clearly on the board or overhead. Every once in a while, before erasing the board or removing an overhead at the end of class, walk to the back and check the legibility of your work from the students' point of view.

5. Put in writing every agreement or accommodation you make with a student, whether it's letting them take a test at a time other than scheduled or allowing them to turn in homework late (be sure to give an exact deadline).

6. Be specific with directions or policies.

7. Encourage students to work together. Give them a chance to practice skills before leaving the classroom and have them work in pairs. There's a great deal to learn through teaching. Give your students this opportunity.

Luke Dowell, *Seward County Community College*

1. Plan the entire semester before it begins. I hand out a "map" that lists when we will cover each section, when things are due, and when the tests will be. This prevents any students from saying they didn't know there was a test. You always have to be flexible, but having a plan keeps you going.

2. Get to know each of your students individually. Try to learn their names by the second or third class period, then use their names in class. I have found that the students who drop a class almost never make connections with the teacher or the other students. If you as the teacher take an interest in them by simply learning their names, they will be more likely to come to you for help instead of dropping out. However, if students still drop, don't take it personally.

3. Let the students know your expectations early and often. If you want homework done a certain way, make it clear. If you don't accept late work, make that clear and stick to it on the very first assignment you pick up. It is okay to have exceptions to your rules, but if you don't stick to your rules and policies early, students can take advantage of it. This is also true about class behavior; if you let things slide early, you might find it hard to get things done later on.

4. Students have a better chance of retaining information if they can link it to other things they already know. Therefore, I like to share the big picture as often as possible with students. For example, the main focus of this text is functions and what you can do with them. When we talk about different types of functions, we deal with what the graph looks like, how to solve equations or inequalities involving that type of function, and modeling applications using that type of function. A good number of the concepts in the text deal with one of those aspects of functions. I remind students of that to help them see where this new material fits in.

5. Any real-world examples of the types of problems you are studying are always helpful to give students a context for the concepts.

Nicki Feldman, *Pulaski Technical College*

1. Many students are math phobic! It only takes one bad math experience to turn them off the discipline for a lifetime. Be positive and encouraging. I often tell my students that I am no smarter than they are, I just have a few more math classes under my belt! Remember, the goal of teaching is not to show the students how much you know, but to explain the concepts in a such a manner that they can synthesize the subject matter, thus being able to show you what they know.

2. Whether you are going to grade homework or not, always assign it! Typically students are unsuccessful even with the greatest instruction unless they practice! Students are a lot more likely to do the homework if it is graded or has some sort of points associated with it. While physical time constraints will not let you grade every problem of every student's homework, come up with a strategy to let the students know you will be checking it. Many of our instructors give a short notebook quiz along with each test. They randomly choose a few homework problems that have been assigned. The students can only use notebooks to copy the problem along with the correct answer. It doesn't take long for them to do or the instructor to grade.

3. Encourage your students to read the text before your lecture. The second time revisiting the material will make a difference. Try to use different examples than those of the text. The students have those to fall back on after you teach your material.

4. Of the 7000+ students at our college, the mean age is 27. Most of our older students have never worked with a graphing calculator. The graphing calculator manual that accompanies this book is excellent! Have students read this and work the examples in the book using the correct keystrokes given step by step in the manual. It is also a good idea when going over problems using the graphing calculator to use an overhead, presenter, or even a poster as a visual aid.

Bridgette L. Jacob, *Onondaga Community College*

1. Make sure to check on the required content for the course you are about to teach for the first time.

2. Ask a seasoned instructor of the course for feedback on your syllabus before the course begins. This will ensure that all necessary items are included and that your policies are reasonable for this course.

3. Once you have set your policies for a course in a particular semester (i.e., attendance, homework, grading, etc.), stick to them. If you feel that changes should be made, you can do that the following semester.

4. Arrive on time for class and return graded materials promptly. You would expect nothing less from your students.

5. Create an atmosphere where anyone can ask a question at any time and answer all questions thoughtfully. Student questions are a wonderful tool to assess their progress.

6. Don't be afraid to let students know that you love mathematics and love teaching it. Show them with your enthusiasm.

7. For this course, require students to bring their graphing calculators to each class.

Renée M. Macaluso, *Arizona Western College*

1. The hardest part about teaching for the first time for me was finding my own teaching style. I received a lot of good advice from great teachers but it was difficult for me to visualize myself doing a lot of the things that other people did (let alone actually doing it). That being said, I won't give a lot of advice. However, I will share a couple of tips that someone can use if the tips appeal to him/her.

2. Something I always struggled with when I started teaching was getting students' attention. Here is what works for me. I often begin the class by sharing a short story, like the morning the neighbor across the street and I backed into each other when we backed out of our driveways. Sometimes I just do something silly, like play the obnoxious elk bugle ring tone on my phone that my brother text messaged me. As long as you don't allow the story to take more than a couple of minutes, it is very effective in getting the students' attention so that you can begin class.

3. Another thing I do that helps me a lot is use PowerPoints during lecture. The PowerPoints only have key points or examples on them but it keeps me focused and organized in class and the students can clearly see what we are working on. I make them available to students in Blackboard so that they can view/print them before class or look at them to see what they missed when they were absent.

Caroline Martinson, *Jefferson Community College*

1. Get to know the calculator background of the students in your class. Those who have used a graphing calculator for four years in high school may be the ones who can mentor the others who have only seen their children use a graphing calculator! Some students have told me it was "like learning algebra and graphing calculator usage at the same time." Balancing assessments with algebraic solutions and graphical solutions has worked well both for me and students.

2. Every semester I seem to have more material than class time. I often limit the work with polynomial functions and severely summarize the material on conics. I use the time gained to spend sufficient time with exponential and logarithmic functions. Exponential and logarithmic functions are new topics for my students. Additionally, my chemistry faculty really want the students to have a firm grasp of the basics of logarithms. The way they explain it, the chemistry instructors don't need to teach logarithms, but just remind the students that "here's the place we'll use them."

3. When I first started using this book, I didn't even look at MathXL. Now I cannot imagine how the students and I got along without it. If you do not know the capabilities of MyMathLab and MathXL, set aside a few hours before you complete your syllabus to explore the potential for this software. I have found this to be one of the best resources the students can have outside the classroom. By moving appropriate tasks to MathXL, I have class time to focus on building stronger critical thinking skills required by the "discussion and writing" and "synthesis" problems found at the end of each section. I require students to "turn in" a set of problems on MathXL before they come to class. I can readily analyze which concepts (if any) caused the most trouble to students and adapt the daily lesson plan accordingly. Consider the computer resources available to your students (personal and on campus) and then decide how you will integrate this feature into your course design.

Pavel Sikorskii, *Michigan State University*

1. Prepare a course syllabus with a day-by-day schedule, assigned homework, a detailed description of the types of graded assignments to be given (such as final exam, tests, quizzes, worksheets, etc.), and an explanation of how the grades will be assigned.

2. Have frequent discussions about the course with other instructors who are currently teaching the course or have taught it in the past.

3. Be prepared for your lectures.

4. Read the textbook and make sure that the notation you are using in class is consistent with the text.

5. Use applications to illustrate how important and useful mathematics is.

6. Try to get students involved and make sure that students are comfortable asking you questions during the lecture.

7. Do not deviate from course policies regarding make-ups and absences. (I found that it is best to have the policies described in the course syllabus.)

8. Make sure that graded assignments are returned to students in a timely fashion and that grading is uniform.

9. Do not make promises you can't keep.

10. Keep accurate records.

11. Make yourself available to students for help outside the classroom and encourage them to take advantage of that.

12. Encourage your students to work in groups.

13. Relax and have fun! Teaching is a rewarding experience!

SAMPLE SYLLABUS

Provided by:

Bridgette L. Jacob, *Onondaga Community College*

College Algebra

3 Credit Hours

INSTRUCTOR: Professor B. Jacob

Office: M210M
Phone and voice mail: xxxx
email: xxxxxx

Office Hours: Mon and Wed 10:00 – 11:00
Tues and Thurs 1:00 – 2:00
(Others by appointment)

DESCRIPTION:

Topics include: Polynomial and absolute value inequalities, functions and their inverses, operations on functions, graphs and transformations, exponential and logarithmic functions, complex numbers, elementary theory of equations, systems of equations, and the binomial theorem. Graphing calculator use is required. Prerequisite: Intermediate Algebra, College Algebra or equivalent.

TEXT:

Precalculus with Trigonometry (Custom Edition for Onondaga Community College) by Bittinger, Beecher, Ellenbogen, and Penna. Pearson Custom Publishing.

The textbook must be purchased through the OCC Bookstore. Note: Make sure to purchase the textbook packaged with the MyMathLab/Course Compass access code.

CALCULATORS:

A graphing calculator is required. The TI-84 Plus or TI-83 Plus are recommended.

ATTENDANCE POLICY:

Students are expected to attend class regularly and attendance will be taken daily. Seven (7) absences with no communication may result in removal from class by Administrative X.

HOMEWORK:

Students are expected to complete all assigned problems. Bring any homework questions to the next class.

EXAMS:

Four (4) unit exams will be given, one at the completion of each unit, and announced a week prior. **No make-up exams will be given.** A two-hour comprehensive exam will be given during finals week.

GRADING POLICY:

Grade	Point Range
A	1258 – 1360
A-	1217 – 1257
B+	1176 – 1216
B	1122 – 1175
B-	1081 – 1121
C+	1040 – 1080
C	986 – 1039
C-	945 – 985
D	809 – 944
F	less than 809

This grading scale is based on the following point distribution:

Thought Questions	60
Homework	600
Exams/Quizzes	500
Final Exam	200
Total Points:	**1360**

COURSE OUTLINE:

Unit One:

1.1   Introduction to Graphing

1.2   Functions and Graphs

1.3   Linear Functions, Slope, and Applications (optional)

1.4   Equations of Lines and Modeling (optional)

1.5   Linear Equations, Functions, Zeros, and Models (optional)

1.6   Solving Linear Inequalities

2.1   Increasing, Decreasing, and Piecewise Functions; Applications

2.2   The Algebra of Functions

2.3   The Composition of Functions

2.4   Symmetry and Transformations

2.5   Variation and Applications (optional)

Unit Two:

3.1   The Complex Numbers

3.2   Quadratic Equations, Functions, Zeros, and Models

3.3   Analyzing Graphs of Quadratic Functions

3.4   Solving Rational and Radical Equations

3.5   Solving Absolute Value Equations and Inequalities

4.1   Polynomial Functions and Modeling

4.2   Graphing Polynomial Functions

4.3   Polynomial Division; The Remainder and Factor Theorems

4.4   Theorems about Zeroes of Polynomial Functions

4.5   Rational Functions (optional)

4.6   Polynomial and Rational Inequalities

Unit Three:

5.1   Inverse Functions

5.2   Exponential Functions and Graphs

5.3   Logarithmic Functions and Graphs

5.4   Properties of Logarithmic Functions

5.5   Solving Exponential and Logarithmic Equations

5.6   Applications and Models: Growth and Decay, and Compound Interest

Unit Four:

6.1   Trigonometric Functions of Acute Angles (from Precalculus)

6.2   Applications of Right Triangles (from Precalculus)

8.1   Sequences and Series

8.7   The Binomial Theorem

STUDENTS WITH SPECIAL NEEDS:

The Disability Services Office (DSO) at Onondaga Community College is available to assist students who have a documented disability. If you require special accommodations for this class, visit the DSO in Room 130 in the Gordon Student Center or call them at xxxxxx. In addition, please see me to discuss your individual circumstances concerning this course.

TEACHING TIPS CORRELATED TO TEXTBOOK SECTIONS

The following is a listing of the objectives, as well as specific teaching tips provided by the contributing professors.

Teaching Tips

Chapter R

I don't actually cover the review chapter. I give the students a page of review problems the second day of class. They turn it in at the end of class and I give them a page with the solutions so that they can see how they did and what they need to go over on their own. I keep their papers so that I can see the class' strengths and weaknesses and review where necessary throughout the semester.

Renée M. Macaluso, *Arizona Western College*

■ ■ ■

I encourage students to take the time to work all the review exercises at the end of this chapter during the first week of class. Questions about these problems are addressed in my office, on MathXL, or in the math learning lab. If students have trouble with a basic skill later in the semester, I often refer them to the necessary part of the review chapter. I don't have time to reteach it all.

Caroline Martinson, *Jefferson Community College*

Section R.1

Reproduce the table on page 4 (or something similar) for your lecture. For many students, this is the first exposure to interval notation. Explain through multiple examples how an inequality, interval notation, and number line graph can display the same information.

Tim Chappell, *Penn Valley Community College*

■ ■ ■

I like to add a problem during class that involves all real numbers except a single number: $\{x \mid x \neq 2\}$, for example.

Amy Del Medico, *Waubonsee Community College*

■ ■ ■

Chapter R
Basic Concepts of Algebra

Objectives

R.1 The Real-Number System

- Identify various kinds of real numbers.
- Use interval notation to write a set of numbers.
- Identify the properties of real numbers.
- Find the absolute value of a real number.

R.2 Integer Exponents, Scientific Notation, and Order of Operations

- Simplify expressions with integer exponents.
- Solve problems using scientific notation.
- Use the rules for order of operations.

R.3 Addition, Subtraction, and Multiplication of Polynomials

- Identify the terms, coefficients, and degree of a polynomial.
- Add, subtract, and multiply polynomials.

R.4 Factoring

- Factor polynomials by removing a common factor.
- Factor polynomials by grouping.
- Factor trinomials of the type $x^2 + bx + c$.
- Factor trinomials of the type $ax^2 + bx + c$, $a \neq 1$, using the FOIL method and the grouping method.
- Factor special products of polynomials.

Teaching Tips

I like to explain the sets of numbers in the context of what students learned as they learned numbers—counting numbers, then zero, then negatives, fractions, etc. I also point out that we need new types of numbers when we learn new operations. For example, whole numbers are enough if you only add or multiply them. When you subtract, you need integers to represent the answers to some problems. When you divide, you need fractions, or rational numbers. Thus students see how we build new concepts onto ones we already know in much the same way they learned new types of numbers and operations as they grew older.

Luke Dowell, *Seward County Community College*

Section R.2

Remind students that a negative exponent means the reciprocal. Suggest the converting of negative exponents before applying the other properties of exponents.

Suggest simple canceling as an alternate method of simplifying the quotient.

Tim Chappell, *Penn Valley Community College*

■ ■ ■

The mortgage-payment problems in this section are a great opportunity to discuss order of operations.

Amy Del Medico, *Waubonsee Community College*

Section R.3

Stress the importance of the square of a binomial. I tell students that it was OK in previous classes to write the binomial twice and use FOIL to get the product. However, it is used in too many ways in College Algebra to go through that each time. I go over several examples, focus homework on this product, and then give a simple quiz the next class period.

Tim Chappell, *Penn Valley Community College*

Section R.4

Reiterate the importance of the square of a binomial.

It is amazing that factoring is, in my opinion, overemphasized in pre-College Algebra courses, and yet students still struggle with factoring. Keep the presentation straightforward and simple.

Tim Chappell, *Penn Valley Community College*

■ ■ ■

Students should see that factoring is essentially the reverse of multiplying two (or more) polynomials together, i.e., $3x(x + 2)$ is the completely factored form of $3x^2 + 6x$. It is also necessary to mention that the largest common factor needs to be removed first, if possible, for each factoring problem.

Betty Larson, *South Dakota State University*

Teaching Tips

Section R.5

I emphasize the difference between an equation and an expression.

Tim Chappell, Penn Valley Community College

Section R.6

It is important that the instructor distinguish between terms and factors. One common error students make is to divide out common terms rather than common factors when simplifying rational expressions or when multiplying or dividing rational expressions.

Example of what *not* to do:

$$\frac{2x^2 + x - 6 -}{x^2 + x - 2 -} \cdot \frac{x^2 - 3x + 2 +}{4x^2 - 6x -}$$

In addition, remind students that as long as the factor occurs in both the denominator and numerator, the factor can be divided out.

Example:

$$\frac{2x^2 + x - 6}{x^2 + x - 2} \cdot \frac{x^2 - 3x + 2}{4x^2 - 6x} = \frac{(2x - 3)(x + 2)}{(x + 2)(x - 1)} \cdot \frac{(x - 2)(x - 1)}{2x(2x - 3)} =$$

$$\frac{(2x - 3)(x + 2)(x - 2)(x - 1)}{(x + 2)(x - 1)2x(2x - 3)} = \frac{\cancel{(2x - 3)}\cancel{(x + 2)}(x - 2)\cancel{(x - 1)}}{\cancel{(x + 2)}\cancel{(x - 1)}2x\cancel{(2x - 3)}}$$

$$= \frac{x - 2}{2x}$$

Marc D. Campbell, Daytona Beach Community College

■ ■ ■

The process of multiplication and division of rational expressions usually goes well for students; it's the factoring that still gets some of them.

For addition and subtraction, go slowly and use different colors in your presentation to show the building up of each fraction.

Tim Chappell, Penn Valley Community College

■ ■ ■

It is worth the time it takes to review how and why canceling works with rational number examples.

Amy Del Medico, Waubonsee Community College

Section R.7

I always use several examples from the Pythagorean theorem to focus on the relevance of radicals.

I do remodeling, and I talk about how to bring out a wall perpendicular to an exterior basement wall.

If a quarterback is 10 yards from the sideline at the 25-yard line and he throws a pass to a receiver 25 yards from the same sideline at the 45-yard line, how far did he throw the ball?

I always present one example of rationalizing the denominator or numerator with an index of three or more and at least one variable factor. I think it helps students understand what it means to rationalize.

Tim Chappell, Penn Valley Community College

R.5 The Basics of Equation Solving

- Solve linear equations.
- Solve quadratic equations.

R.6 Rational Expressions

- Determine the domain of a rational expression.
- Simplify rational expressions.
- Multiply, divide, add, and subtract rational expressions.
- Simplify complex rational expressions.

R.7 Radical Notation and Rational Exponents

- Simplify radical expressions.
- Rationalize denominators or numerators in rational expressions.
- Convert between exponential and radical notation.
- Simplify expressions with rational exponents.

Chapter 1
Graphs, Functions, and Inequalities

Objectives

1.1 Introduction to Graphing

- Plot points.
- Determine whether an ordered pair is a solution of an equation.
- Graph equations.
- Find the distance between two points in the plane and find the midpoint of a segment.
- Find an equation of a circle with a given center and radius, and given an equation of a circle, find the center and the radius.
- Graph equations of circles.

1.2 Functions and Graphs

- Determine whether a correspondence or a relation is a function.
- Find function values, or outputs, using a formula.
- Determine whether a graph is that of a function.
- Find the domain and the range of a function.
- Solve applied problems using functions.

Teaching Tips

Section 1.1

When finding the center point of a circle, that is, h and k, have the students rewrite the quantities $(x + 1)^2$ and $(y - 2)^2$:

$$(x + 1)^2 = [x - (-1)]^2, \text{ so } h = -1$$
$$(y - 2)^2 = [y - (2)]^2, \text{ so } k = 2.$$

Marc D. Campbell, Daytona Beach Community College

■ ■ ■

Students miss the midpoint formula because they subtract instead of add. Require that they graph the three points or at least verify that the midpoint's coordinates are in the middle of the endpoints' coordinates.

Tim Chappell, Penn Valley Community College

■ ■ ■

There is a lot of information in this section. I suggest breaking the section into two parts, the first day being all the work without a graphing calculator. Many of our students have never worked with a graphing calculator before this course. In addition to the homework I assign on the first day, I make a heavy reading/exploring assignment from the review chapter with the graphing calculator. This will give students a little time to start learning the keystrokes of the calculator. Emphasize that the graphing calculator manual follows the examples in the book, and shows the correct keystrokes step by step. In the next class it really helps to have a poster and/or overhead of the graphing calculator to help the students follow along.

Nicki Feldman, Pulaski Technical College

■ ■ ■

If the graphing calculator is an integral part of the course, it is a good idea to get the students acclimated to it right from the start. Finding the best viewing window is a difficult task for many. Encourage students to use the TABLE feature to help by observing corresponding input and output values.

Bridgette L. Jacob, Onondaga Community College

Section 1.2

Here, I introduce the basic elementary graphs. That is, $f(x) = x$, $f(x) = x^2$, $f(x) = x^3$, $f(x) = |x|$, $f(x) = \sqrt{x}$, and $f(x) = \sqrt[3]{x}$. Likewise, I introduce the reflection about the x-axis. I think it is very important that the student memorize the function along with its graph. This makes symmetry and transformation go much smoother. Students can focus solely on symmetry and transformations and not have to wonder or ask, "How did you know the graph of that equation looks like that?" To further enforce the importance of these, I give a matching and fill-in-the-blank quiz on basic functions and their graphs.

Marc D. Campbell, Daytona Beach Community College

■ ■ ■

Teaching Tips

Focus on the graphical and numerical representations of functions using finite sets before going into the algebra. Emphasize the importance of functions in our lives.

Tim Chappell, *Penn Valley Community College*

■ ■ ■

This is another section that I spend a couple of class periods covering, not because of the length of the section, but because students struggle with the concepts of domain and range. I spend extra time on domain and range and give them examples to work in class and turn in.

Renée M. Macaluso, *Arizona Western College*

■ ■ ■

Function notation and function evaluation can be tricky. I use parentheses as place holders instead of variables so that students get a better feel for the input/output concept, i.e., $f(x) = 2x^2 + 3x - 5$ is rewritten as $f(\ ) = 2(\ )^2 + 3(\ ) - 5$. Using an overhead with this adjusted function notation on one sheet and then a blank sheet on top that is used for the input/output is very effective.

Amy Del Medico, *Waubonsee Community College*

■ ■ ■

Using real-world examples of functions helps drive home the concept of what a function is. In the past I have had students cut out examples of functions from newspapers or magazines. They did not have to be numerical examples. Also, stressing the fact that $f(x)$ takes the place of y helps students understand what function notation is all about.

Luke Dowell, *Seward Country Community College*

■ ■ ■

Relating the graphical representation of a function to the equation of the function is important in this course. Students find it difficult to visualize the domain and range from the graph of a function, so spend extra time helping them do this.

Bridgette L. Jacob, *Onondaga Community College*

■ ■ ■

Function notation is new to some students. I stress that students MUST be able to determine from $f(7) = 1$ the input value and the output value of the function. I also stress the fact that the domain of a function does NOT include any value that makes a denominator zero or the radicand of a square root negative. We come back to this many times throughout the semester!

Caroline Martinson, *Jefferson Community College*

1.3 Linear Functions, Slope, and Applications

- Determine the slope of a line given two points on the line.
- Solve applied problems involving slope and linear functions.

Teaching Tips

Section 1.3

This is arguably the most important concept in college mathematics. Slope is covered in all levels of algebra as well as in Calculus and in most other disciplines through regression analysis. Emphasize the meaning of subscripts and their use in math before presenting the slope formula. I ask my students to explain slope in terms a non-math person would understand. Slope is essentially the relationship (ratio) between the change in something and the change in something else. Students then come up with an example of slope meaningful to them (major, hobby, etc.) that we discuss during the first 10 minutes of the next class period. Although it is not in the book, I also ask student to be able to generate additional points given a point and a slope using the concept of slope.

Tim Chappell, *Penn Valley Community College*

■ ■ ■

Many students have worked with linear equations or functions before, but they have difficulty with some of the applications. When the task requires writing the linear function that models a particular problem, they find it difficult to establish the two points needed from the wording of the problem.

Bridgette L. Jacob, *Onondaga Community College*

■ ■ ■

I begin this section by asking the students what comes to mind when they hear the word slope, not necessarily in a math setting. This begins a class discussion about ski slopes, pitches of roofs, grades of roads, etc. I then relate those ideas to the mathematical definition of slope. However, the students usually do not volunteer slope as a rate of change when I ask for their thoughts on slope and so we spend time then talking about slope as a rate of change.

Renée M. Macaluso, *Arizona Western College*

■ ■ ■

Many students finally have an "aha" moment when we carefully discuss linear functions as having a constant rate of change (slope). When the x-values increase (decrease) by a constant amount, the y-values also demonstrate a constant change. We look at the linear and nonlinear data sets found in this section. There is a constant difference in the x-values for both sets of data. In the linear data set, the difference in y-values is also constant. Therefore, the data represent a linear function. I alert students that when we get to Section 3.2 we will revisit the nonlinear data. However, we look at it now to see why it is nonlinear. Students agree that the data are nonlinear since the y-values do not have a constant rate of change the first time we subtract. I suggest that we now subtract a second time, and look at that! In the second subtraction all the differences are the same. Could these be data that will "fit" some second-degree equation? Hmmm . . .

I emphasize that the y-intercept is a point. The y-intercept is not 5, but rather the point $(0, 5)$, a point on the y-axis.

I use (x, y) and (h, k) as two points to derive a general form of the equation of a line as $y = m(x - h) + k$. For me this clearly connects all general forms of algebraic descriptions for some other relations: circles, quadratics, and conics.

Caroline Martinson, *Jefferson Community College*

Teaching Tips

Section 1.4

We cover this topic as a project. Students find or collect data for two variables that they feel have a linear or fairly linear relationship, and they develop a short paper.

Tim Chappell, Penn Valley Community College

■ ■ ■

For the sections on regression analysis I create a handout with the step-by-step process to hand out to my students. The students are then able to concentrate more on the purpose and analysis rather than on remembering what button to push next on their calculators.

Amy Del Medico, Waubonsee Community College

■ ■ ■

I got a much better response on this section when I brought in my own data and told students to help me answer my own questions using the data. For example, one semester I asked students to tell me if there was a correlation between the number of days a student missed class and his or her grade in class. Then I let them gather their own data and ask their own questions about the relationship between quantities. This seemed to make this concept more accessible to students.

Luke Dowell, Seward County Community College

■ ■ ■

A quick review of algebraic techniques will help students to write a linear equation in slope-intercept form, if it is not already, to easily determine the slope and y-intercept. When modeling a set of data, the concept of using zero (0) to represent the initial year or time is confusing for students. It may be worth class time to demonstrate an example using the full year, 1970 for example, and then the zero representation for the initial year. It is important for them to understand that either representation will generate a viable modeling equation.

Bridgette L. Jacob, Onondaga Community College

■ ■ ■

This is another long section that I spend a couple of classes covering. The first class is spent on the equations of lines and then the second day is spent covering curve fitting. I like to bring in real data to use. I have used data like the enrollment in AWC math classes over several years and my church's average monthly attendance over several years. If I don't have recent real data on hand, we work homework problems from this section as a class.

Renée M. Macaluso, Arizona Western College

■ ■ ■

Some students are using a calculator that does not give the correlation coefficient, so I do not ask for that value. I will, however, expect all students to be able to determine when the data have a high or low, positive or negative correlation.

Caroline Martinson, Jefferson Community College

1.4 Equations of Lines and Modeling

- Find the slope and the y-intercept of a line given the equation $y = mx + b$, or $f(x) = mx + b$.
- Graph a linear equation using the slope and the y-intercept.
- Determine equations of lines.
- Given the equations of two lines, determine whether their graphs are parallel or whether they are perpendicular.
- Model a set of data with a linear function.
- Fit a regression line to a set of data; then use the linear model to make predictions.

1.5 Linear Equations, Functions, Zeros, and Models

- Solve linear equations.
- Solve applied problems using linear models.
- Find zeros of linear functions.
- Solve a formula for a given variable.

Teaching Tips

Section 1.5

At this point, I reinforce the definition of a function and teach students how to determine if an equation is a relation or a function. I do the same with graphs.

Marc D. Campbell, *Daytona Beach Community College*

■ ■ ■

Students like this section when I explain that they will be allowed to check all solutions to equations with their graphing calculator.

Tim Chappell, *Penn Valley Community College*

■ ■ ■

Most students can comprehend the material in this section. I emphasize finding the zero on the calculator, which will help tremendously in future sections if it is mastered here.

Nicki Feldman, *Pulaski Technical College*

■ ■ ■

While students work through the linear modeling questions, it is a good time to familiarize them with the graphing calculator functions of ZERO and INTERSECT as well as the TABLE feature. This will be a tremendous help for the students as they proceed through the course.

Bridgette L. Jacob, *Onondaga Community College*

■ ■ ■

Students often avoid even attempting word problems. To get them to attempt at least a couple of application problems, I have them try some problems in class to turn in to me (after I've done a few examples). They are allowed to work together and I don't grade the problems for accuracy. They simply get credit for attempting problems, but I do correct their work before giving it back to them.

Renée M. Macaluso, *Arizona Western College*

1.6 Solving Linear Inequalities

- Solve linear inequalities.
- Solve compound inequalities.
- Solve applied problems using inequalities.

Section 1.6

When solving any type of inequality, I use the test point method. Students like it because once you have learned the test point method, you can use it to solve any type of inequality.

1: Solve the related equation.
2: Put the solutions on a number line.
3: Pick a number from each interval on the number line.
   a) If it makes the original inequality true, the interval is part of the solution,
   b) If it makes the original inequality false, the interval is not part of the solution.

Marc D. Campbell, *Daytona Beach Community College*

■ ■ ■

Interval notation, once again, is important here. Make sure that students understand that they can also check their answers for these inequalities by substituting a value **within** an interval rather than at the endpoint of an interval.

Bridgette L. Jacob, *Onondaga Community College*

Teaching Tips

Section 2.1

I find most students have trouble combining piecewise linear functions graphically. I usually refer them to Section 1.2 to revisit graphical representations of functions.

Tim Chappell, *Penn Valley Community College*

■ ■ ■

I use storytelling to illustrate the concepts of increasing and decreasing functions as well as relative maxima and minima. The story I use is of a mountain climber, and say we would like to record his mountain climbing trip. The graph of the function is the picture of the mountains he climbs with the horizontal mile markers along the x-axis and his "altitude" on the y-axis.

Amy Del Medico, *Waubonsee Community College*

■ ■ ■

I use real-world examples to help students see where piecewise functions are used. Many phone plans can be modeled using piecewise functions.

Luke Dowell, *Seward County Community College*

■ ■ ■

Many instructors break this section into two days to make sure all the material is covered. This information will be used over and over throughout the rest of the text, and it is important that the students have correct comprehension of this material. I suggest breaking the section at piecewise functions. In teaching piecewise functions, I like to make sure the students understand that the domain of each "piece" of the function is limited. I stress doing these by hand until the concept is mastered. It is a great review of their earlier algebra classes and the graphing methods used.

Nicki Feldman, *Pulaski Technical College*

■ ■ ■

The difficulty for students here is not in finding the intervals of increase or decrease, but in the notation for these intervals. When to use parentheses and when to use brackets is such an important concept for them to grasp, especially if they are headed into a calculus course. This is important also for the piecewise-defined functions. The proper graphical representation of a piecewise function will go a long way in helping students to understand whether or not an endpoint is actually included in an interval or not. This graphical representation will also assist students in determining a particular function value. Which "piece" of the piecewise function to use for a given input is confusing for them as well.

Bridgette L. Jacob, *Onondaga Community College*

■ ■ ■

Chapter 2
More on Functions

Objectives

2.1 Increasing, Decreasing, and Piecewise Functions; Applications

- Graph functions, looking for intervals on which the function is increasing, decreasing, or constant, and estimate relative maxima and minima.

- Given an application, find a function that models the application, find the domain of the function and function values, and then graph the function.

- Graph functions defined piecewise.

Students struggle with setting up word problems. We spend quite a bit of time talking about how to set them up. After doing several examples, we look for the common theme. The first is to write a general formula for whatever it is that they're asked to find a function for, without worrying about how many variables are being used in the formula. Then, they need to write all the variables in the formula in terms of the single desired variable using other information from the problem. Once they get past those two steps, they don't struggle as much with the rest of the problem.

Renée M. Macaluso, *Arizona Western College*

■ ■ ■

The text gives an example of a piece-wise defined function where one piece of the function is a rational function. I make sure students know WHY there is a "hole" in the graph. Also, for students who have never encountered the greatest integer function, the text provides a good explanation.

Caroline Martinson, *Jefferson Community College*

2.2 The Algebra of Functions

- Find the sum, the difference, the product, and the quotient of two functions, and determine the domains of the resulting functions.
- Find the difference quotient for a function.

Section 2.2

What I have found to be the biggest pitfall when talking to students about operations on functions is the mathematical notation. So my initial approach is as follows:

Example: Given two polynomials A and B, let $A = -3 + 5x$ and $B = 5 - 7x$. Find $A + B$, $A - B$, AB, and A/B. All college algebra students should be able to do this. Once they have finished, I go back and replace A with $f(x)$ and B with $g(x)$. Now they have $f(x) = -3 + 5x$ and $g(x) = 5 - 7x$. Then I tell them to find $f(x) + g(x)$ and so on and then, using the same functions, tell them to find $(f + g)(x)$ and so on. Almost in one voice, they all will say, "It's the same." At this point, your students will realize that $f(x) + g(x)$ and $(f + g)(x)$ mean the same thing, adding functions.

Marc D. Campbell, *Daytona Beach Community College*

■ ■ ■

I emphasize reading graphs. Given the graphs of f and g (no equations), evaluate $(f + g)(2)$, $g(f(-1))$, find the domain and range of f/g, etc.

Pavel Sikorskii, *Michigan State University*

Teaching Tips

Section 2.3

When dealing with composite functions, I take my students through a series of examples. Through these examples, we discover the mathematical definition and procedure of doing composite functions.

If $f(x) = 2x + 1$, evaluate this function when

$$x = 1 \rightarrow f(1) = 2(1) + 1 = 3$$
$$x = -2 \rightarrow f(-2) = 2(-2) + 1 = -3$$
$$x = a \rightarrow f(a) = 2(a) + 1 = 2a + 1$$
$$x = g \rightarrow f(g) = 2(g) + 1 = 2g + 1.$$

At this point, everyone can see the substitution process. Now, look at the last of the functions evaluated:

$$f(g) = 2(g) + 1 = 2g + 1.$$

Tell your students to replace g with $x + 1$ and see what happens.

$$g = x + 1 \rightarrow f(x + 1) = 2(x + 1) + 1 = 2x + 2 + 1 = 2x + 3$$

Now explain by that substituting $x + 1$ for g, they (the students) have done a composition of functions. That is, for $f(x) = 2x + 1$ and $g(x) = x + 1$, $f(g(x)) = f(x + 1) = 2(x + 1) + 1 = 2x + 3$.

Marc D. Campbell, *Daytona Beach Community College*

■ ■ ■

We discuss multi-step functions, such as assembly lines, crafts, etc., as examples of composite functions.

Tim Chappell, *Penn Valley Community College*

■ ■ ■

Make a very clear distinction in the difference between a product of functions and a composition of functions. Often students confuse the two notations and revert to multiplication.

Bridgette L. Jacob, *Onondaga Community College*

■ ■ ■

We spend most of our time on the composition and decomposition of functions since students struggle with those more. Also, I emphasize the difference quotient.

Renée M. Macaluso, *Arizona Western College*

2.3 The Composition of Functions

- Find the composition of two functions and the domain of the composition; decompose a function as a composition of two functions.

2.4 Symmetry and Transformations

- Determine whether a graph is symmetric with respect to the x-axis, the y-axis, and the origin.
- Determine whether a function is even, odd, or neither even nor odd.
- Given the graph of a function, graph its transformation under translations, reflections, stretchings, and shrinkings.

Teaching Tips

Section 2.4

Before giving my students the mathematical definition of symmetry, I talk about symmetry as it relates to the quadrants and axes. I tell my students, when talking about symmetry with respect to the x-axis, look above and below the x-axis (for a mirror image). When talking about symmetry with respect to the y-axis, look to the left and right of the y-axis (for a mirror image). When talking about symmetry with respect to the origin, look at the diagonals (for a mirror image). And to reinforce the basic elementary graphs, I talk about the symmetry that I mentioned earlier as it related to the basic elementary graphs.

I have had great success in having my students memorize the transformations because I teach them in steps. That is, students have already learned the basic functions with their graphs (1.2). So, in one day of lecture, I will talk about the vertical shift and run through that with each basic elementary graph, and also talk about the horizontal shift and run through that with each basic elementary graph. After that, I do a couple of examples combining the two shifts. After that, I do a couple of examples with a vertical shift, a horizontal shift, and a reflection about the x-axis. To conclude that day's lesson, I would mention reflection about the y-axis and what it looks like, but by that time most students have caught on.

Marc D. Campbell, *Daytona Beach Community College*

■ ■ ■

Vertical and horizontal translations can be thought of as adjustments to the function on the "outside" and "inside" respectively. This also applies to reflections and stretching/shrinking. If anything (adding, subtracting, multiplying) is done "outside" the basic function, then it will have a vertical effect. If the operation occurs "inside," then the effect is horizontal in nature. It helps the students to remember the effect of each of the transformations if they are broken down into two main groups first.

Amy Del Medico, *Waubonsee Community College*

■ ■ ■

I have students use graphing calculators and help them discover some of the concepts related to symmetry and transformations. Using the interactive discovery sections in the text really helps with this.

Luke Dowell, *Seward County Community College*

■ ■ ■

I have the students explore on their calculator with a homemade worksheet comparing the graphs of $y = x^2$ and $y = x^2 + 3$. I do this with each of the transformations and draw conclusions at the end. This way the students can tell you what adding or subtracting a number "inside" or "outside" the function will result in and they have derived the rules themselves. It seems to help in comprehension and retention of this material.

Nicki Feldman, *Pulaski Technical College*

■ ■ ■

Teaching Tips

Spend some extra time on the transformations of functions. This is particularly important in developing a student's ability to visualize the basic functions and transformations of each.

Bridgette L. Jacob, *Onondaga Community College*

■ ■ ■

I spend two classes on this section. I open the first day of class with a class discussion about symmetry and where they see it. Then we get into the mathematical definitions. The second class is spent on the transformations of functions. After giving the mathematical definition of the various transformations, we do some examples of each of the transformations individually and then a couple of examples of combinations of transformations of functions. When we do the examples, I give students graphs of the basic graphs and they graph the transformations on the same coordinate axes.

Renée M. Macaluso, *Arizona Western College*

■ ■ ■

This is one of those places where algebraic and graphical representations are equally stressed and strongly connected. Some students have worked through this in many prior courses and this is solely review. For others, however, it is totally new.

Caroline Martinson, *Jefferson Community College*

■ ■ ■

I always make sure that I spend some time convincing the students that the order in which the transformations are performed matters.

Pavel Sikorskii, *Michigan State University*

Section 2.5

This is largely review from prior courses in our curriculum. I make sure all know it, but often do not need to spend much time with examples and explanation.

Caroline Martinson, *Jefferson Community College*

■ ■ ■

Students often understand this concept much better when they are using a formula like $P = Irt$. After changing the values of variables one at a time, the students can determine which variables are directly and inversely related to each other.

Sharon Testone, *Onondaga Community College*

2.5 Variation and Applications

- Find equations of direct, inverse, and combined variation given values of the variables.
- Solve applied problems involving variation.

Chapter 3
Quadratic Functions and Equations; Inequalities

Objectives

3.1 The Complex Numbers

- Perform computations involving complex numbers.

Teaching Tips

Section 3.1

When dealing with complex numbers, I start by telling my students that new does not always mean hard. I give them two polynomials and ask them to perform the basic operations of addition, subtraction, and multiplication. For example, let $A = -3 + 5x$ and $B = 5 - 7x$. Now, find $A + B$, $A - B$, and AB. Once they have finished, I go back and replace x with the letter i and tell them to do the same operations. Almost in one voice, they all will say, "It's the same," and my point is made.

Don't forget—you must still introduce $i = \sqrt{-1}$ and the idea of a conjugate for the division of complex numbers but at least you get them started in a positive direction when it comes to complex numbers.

Marc D. Campbell, *Daytona Beach Community College*

■ ■ ■

Multiplying complex numbers takes FOIL a step further. Students see that the product of the First terms and the product of the Last terms can be combined as well as the product of the Outer terms and the product of the Inner terms.

I emphasize the closure property for complex numbers. Every operation with complex numbers can be simplified down to at most two terms, a term with i to the first power and a constant.

Tim Chappell, *Penn Valley Community College*

■ ■ ■

Although this section is optional at our institution, the students like to cover it. It gives them added success on exams. I teach both by hand and the calculator on this section. It also reviews material we have taught in our developmental classes.

Nicki Feldman, *Pulaski Technical College*

■ ■ ■

Convince students that the product of conjugates will always be a real number by allowing time for them to experiment with this in class. Working through several examples and examining the process, step by step, will help them to understand why this is so.

Bridgette L. Jacob, *Onondaga Community College*

■ ■ ■

I use this opportunity to remind students that the real numbers are just a subset of the complex numbers. Like the text, I point out that when students know what i represents, then they also know what i^2 represents. It is with this small bit of knowledge that students can do all the arithmetic with complex numbers.

Caroline Martinson, *Jefferson Community College*

■ ■ ■

Students usually do well with these. I would suggest an extra example on division and powers of i.

Pavel Sikorskii, *Michigan State University*

Teaching Tips

Section 3.2

When dealing with functions, I try to get my students to see that a zero is another term for a solution of $f(x) = 0$. At this point, students should know that $f(x) = y$, thus finding the zero(s) of a function is done the same way you solve for the x-intercept.

I do an example and put it in chart form for my students showing how zeros, roots, solutions, factors, and x-intercept all are integrated with one another. For example, to find the zeros of $f(x) = x^2 + x - 6$, I have to factor first; that is, $f(x) = (x - 2)(x + 3)$. Thus

1:   2 and -3 are zeros of the function $f(x)$.
2:   2 and -3 are solutions of the equation
     $f(x) = x^2 + x - 6 = 0$.
3:   $(x-2)$ and $(x + 3)$ are factors of $x^2 + x - 6$.
4:   Because $f(2) = 0$ and $f(-3) = 0$ (from step 2), the x-intercepts are $(2, 0)$ and $(-3, 0)$.

Marc D. Campbell, Daytona Beach Community College

■ ■ ■

I use completing the square as a method to develop the quadratic formula, but then I focus on the quadratic formula.

I remind students that if the leading coefficient a is always positive, they should watch the constant c to determine whether the discriminant will involve an subtraction or an addition.

Make sure to include problems on determining whether functions are linear or quadratic. I find students sometimes miss what we as math teachers find trivial.

Tim Chappell, Penn Valley Community College

■ ■ ■

Most of this section is a review for our students. However, some may not have fully grasped the quadratic formula. I like to show the students how the quadratic formula is derived in proof form, and it makes for an excellent bonus question on the test.

Nicki Feldman, Pulaski Technical College

■ ■ ■

Extra practice will be required for students to grasp the concept of completing the square to solve a quadratic equation. A quick review of the multiplication of polynomials and factoring will be helpful.

Bridgette L. Jacob, Onondaga Community College

■ ■ ■

Whenever the quadratic formula is derived/introduced, I cannot resist a short history lesson, or a brief research project. History can make the math more interesting.

Caroline Martinson, Jefferson Community College

■ ■ ■

Review all methods. Emphasize factoring and completing the square!

Pavel Sikorskii, Michigan State University

3.2 Quadratic Equations, Functions, Zeros, and Models

- Find zeros of quadratic functions and solve quadratic equations by using the principle of zero products, by using the principle of square roots, by completing the square, and by using the quadratic formula.
- Solve equations that are reducible to quadratic.
- Solve applied problems using quadratic equations.

3.3 Analyzing Graphs of Quadratic Functions

- Find the vertex, the axis of symmetry, and the maximum or minimum value of a quadratic function using the method of completing the square.
- Graph quadratic functions.
- Solve applied problems involving maximum and minimum function values.

Teaching Tips

Section 3.3

I teach the use of $(-b/(2a), f(-b/(2a)))$ to find the vertex of the parabola.

I like to use examples to introduce the position function, and I assign homework problems that require the position function.

Tim Chappell, *Penn Valley Community College*

■ ■ ■

This section ties together a lot of material that has been learned up to this point. I try to emphasize the transformations in use from Section 2.4, and relate the zeros of the functions from Section 3.2.

Nicki Feldman, *Pulaski Technical College*

■ ■ ■

Students' work with transformations and with completing the square comes together in analyzing the graphs of quadratic functions. Spend time relating the algebraic and graphical representations of quadratics. Once again, interval notation can be emphasized as students find maximums, minimums, and intervals of increase and decrease.

Bridgette L. Jacob, *Onondaga Community College*

■ ■ ■

Here's another place where algebraic analysis and graphical analysis can certainly enhance understanding. I also use this opportunity to compare $y = m(x - h) + k$ to $y = a(x - h)^2 + k$ to $(x - h)^2 + (y - k)^2 = r^2$ to build the connections to what we already know.

Caroline Martinson, *Jefferson Community College*

■ ■ ■

Make the connection with transformations. I also spend a lot of time on applications—this is where students are introduced to optimization problems. I usually spend two lectures on this section.

Pavel Sikorskii, *Michigan State University*

Teaching Tips

Section 3.4

To show why there may be "extraneous solutions" when you square both sides, I begin with a false statement like $-4 = 4$. Then when you square both sides, you get a true statement, $16 = 16$.

For these equations, I encourage checking with a calculator either through graphing or through calculation.

Tim Chappell, Penn Valley Community College

■ ■ ■

Remind students that they can always check their work when solving equations of any type by substituting their answers back into the original equation. If time allows, graphical solutions can be explored with the graphing calculator by graphing the left and right sides of an equation and finding points of intersection.

Bridgette L. Jacob, Onondaga Community College

■ ■ ■

Often the only new material from this section is solving equations with two radicals. I briefly review algebraic solutions of the other types presented in this section. I insist on the skill of obtaining a solution algebraically. I encourage the use of the calculator to "check" your answer.

Caroline Martinson, Jefferson Community College

■ ■ ■

Section 3.5

Consistently remind students that absolute value is a measure of the distance from 0 on the real number line. Work this idea into solving absolute value equations and inequalities. I use the analogy of "staying close to home" while growing up when discussing $|x| < k$. This reinforces the distance concept and gives students something to relate it to.

Amy Del Medico, Waubonsee Community College

■ ■ ■

Algebraic solution of linear and absolute value inequalities is often review for the majority of students in my classes. A brief Q&A time usually has been sufficient.

Caroline Martinson, Jefferson Community College

■ ■ ■

In checking solutions to an inequality, there are two checks to make. First, students need to check to make sure they have the critical point(s) right. Second, they need to check that their interval(s) are correct.

Tim Chappell, Penn Valley Community College

3.4 Solving Rational and Radical Equations

- Solve rational and radical equations.

3.5 Solving Absolute Value Equations and Inequalities

- Solve equations with absolute value.
- Solve inequalities with absolute value.

Chapter 4
Polynomial and Rational Functions

Objectives

4.1 Polynomial Functions and Modeling

- Determine the behavior of the graph of a polynomial function using the leading-term test.
- Factor polynomial functions and find the zeros and their multiplicities.
- Use a graphing calculator to graph a polynomial function and find its real-number zeros, relative maximum and minimum values, and domain and range.
- Solve applied problems using polynomial models; fit linear, quadratic, power, cubic, and quartic polynomial functions to data.

Teaching Tips

Section 4.1

I begin by reviewing graphs of basic quadratic and cubic functions. If the leading coefficient is positive, then you have the curve of the basic elementary graph, and if the leading coefficient is negative, then you have the reflection across the x-axis of the basic elementary graph. Without great detail I introduce the power rule, which states, "The end behavior of any even powered polynomial function will have the same end behavior of a quadratic function" and "The end behavior of any odd powered polynomial function will have the same end behavior of a cubic function." Now you have tied the end behavior of any polynomial to two they already know.

When I tie the leading term test with the power rule, students understand and gain more insight to the end behavior of a polynomial graph.

Marc D. Campbell, Daytona Beach Community College

■ ■ ■

Understanding the end behavior of the graph of a function allows the student to determine if, indeed, they are viewing the entire function in the window of the graphing calculator. If so, then they are able to fully analyze the function.

The multiplicity of a zero of a function is a difficult concept for students. Examining several polynomials graphically with the same zeros and changing multiplicities will be helpful.

Bridgette L. Jacob, Onondaga Community College

■ ■ ■

To sketch the general behavior of a polynomial function, I encourage students to KNOW the graphs of $y = x^2$ and $y = x^3$. Based on a clear understanding of reflections, stretching, and shrinking (from Section 2.4), they have no problem with the effect of the leading coefficient. We compare the graphs of 2nd degree, 4th degree, and 6th degree functions. Students are often able to generalize and can make a prediction about 3rd, 5th, and 7th degree polynomials.

Caroline Martinson, Jefferson Community College

■ ■ ■

Students have usually mastered finding the zeros graphically by this point. I like to emphasize the problems that make the student change the window to see what is happening close to the zeros, minimums, and maximums.

Nicki Feldman, Pulaski Technical College

Teaching Tips

Section 4.2

Sketching graphs of polynomial functions allows students to check their understanding of the connections between the equations of functions and the graphs of those functions.

Bridgette L. Jacob, *Onondaga Community College*

Section 4.3

Develop synthetic division through the long division process. I ask students not to take notes during its development; I want them to clearly follow exactly why it works. Then we jump into the synthetic division problems for the remainder of the class time.

Tim Chappell, *Penn Valley Community College*

■ ■ ■

By using examples, I help students discover these theorems before we read them in the text. A lot of times, we write our own theorems "in English" then look at the text to compare.

Luke Dowell, *Seward County Community College*

■ ■ ■

My students usually struggle with long division in algebra. I remind them to view the steps of long division as an algorithm—daddy, mother, sister, brother—long division is a family affair, for divide, multiply, subtract, and bring down. I further tell them when they divide they will use first terms only. Most of their mistakes come on the subtract step, in forgetting to distribute the negative sign before combining like terms.

Nicki Feldman, *Pulaski Technical College*

■ ■ ■

Synthetic division is difficult for students at first, but as they practice, they then see the benefits of using it. Remind students when using synthetic division for factoring that, after dividing one factor into a polynomial, a second factor is then divided into the *remainder* just obtained. Often students will go back to the original polynomial which leaves them at a loss as to how to factor the polynomial.

Bridgette L. Jacob, *Onondaga Community College*

■ ■ ■

Remember to reiterate the relationship between zeros and factors. To assess understanding of the remainder theorem, I may ask: "Given the function $f(x) = 3x^{53} - 2x^{14} + 6$, what is the remainder when $f(x)$ is divided by $(x - 1)$?" Students get lost in synthetic division instead of realizing there is another way.

Caroline Martinson, *Jefferson Community College*

4.2 Graphing Polynomial Functions

- Graph polynomial functions.
- Use the intermediate value theorem to determine whether a function has a real zero between two given real numbers.

4.3 Polynomial Division; The Remainder and Factor Theorems

- Perform long division with polynomials and determine whether one polynomial is a factor of another.
- Use synthetic division to divide a polynomial by $x - c$.
- Use the remainder theorem to find a function value $f(c)$.
- Use the factor theorem to determine whether $x - c$ is a factor of $f(x)$.

4.4 Theorems about Zeros of Polynomial Functions

- Find a polynomial with specified zeros.
- For a polynomial function with integer coefficients, find the rational zeros and the other zeros, if possible.
- Use Descartes' rule of signs to find information about the number of real zeros of a polynomial function with real coefficients.

Teaching Tips

Section 4.4

Develop the rational zeros theorem by factoring a quadratic polynomial with non-integer zeros, and then tracing where the numerators and denominators of the zeros came from. Students usually remember to divide factors of one number by factors of another number. They just forget which number to use first. I ask them to find the zeros of a simple polynomial like $2x + 5$. Then they can always figure it out without having to memorize rules.

Students don't always multiply in the easiest way to find a polynomial function with the given zeros. We walk through which ones to multiply when for a number of problems, and actually only work out one or two problems of that type.

Tim Chappell, *Penn Valley Community College*

■ ■ ■

I ask the students do this the way we were taught 20+ years ago with all the theorems and no help from the graphing calculator first. Then they really appreciate being able to graph the function to look for the real zeros before doing the synthetic division.

Nicki Feldman, *Pulaski Technical College*

■ ■ ■

Finding the polynomial when given irrational or complex zeros is algebraically difficult for students. Spend some class time demonstrating this and give students time to practice. When given one irrational or complex zero of a polynomial function and asked to find the other, students sometimes give incomplete answers. For example, if one zero is $1 + 5i$, they may give the other as $1 - 5i$.

Bridgette L. Jacob, *Onondaga Community College*

■ ■ ■

Once students know how to find the zeros of a polynomial function and their multiplicity, I ask students to connect the effect of multiplicity of zeros to what we learned in Section 4.2 about the general shape of the graph to make a "better" sketch. Discovery: How does the graph of $f(x) = (x - 1)^2(x + 5)$ compare to $g(x) = (x - 1)(x + 5)^2$? How does the graph of $f(x) = (x - 1)(x + 5)$ compare to $g(x) = (x - 1)(x + 5)^3$? How does the graph of $f(x) = (x - 1)(x + 5)^2$ compare to $g(x) = (x - 1)(x + 5)^4$? In general, explain how the multiplicity of a zero affects the behavior of its related graph. Inevitably the descriptors are bouncing and cutting, hard and soft.

Caroline Martinson, *Jefferson Community College*

■ ■ ■

I would suggest starting with the summary of fundamental theorems about polynomials followed by the large-scale behavior. I spend a significant part of this lecture explaining to the students why the leading term determines the behavior of a polynomial function for large values of x. I also emphasize the intermediate value theorem for polynomials.

Pavel Sikorskii, *Michigan State University*

Teaching Tips

Section 4.5

I have students create a number of rational functions with certain asymptotes that we then graph to see if we are right. I think when students clearly learn what part of a rational function determines each kind of asymptote and intercept, they can pull the information out of a function.

Tim Chappell, *Penn Valley Community College*

■ ■ ■

I have my students make an asymptote summary sheet at the beginning of this section.

3 Types of Asymptotes

1. Vertical
2. Horizontal
3. Oblique or Slant

   1) **Vertical:** (domain) the vertical asymptotes occur at the zeros of the denominator.

   2) **Horizontal:** Compare the function to $y = \dfrac{p(x)}{q(x)}$.

   You must find the degree for both $p(x)$ and $q(x)$.

   1. If the degree of $p(x)$ ‹ the degree of $q(x)$, the horizontal asymptote is $y = 0$.
   2. If the degree of $p(x) =$ the degree of $q(x)$, the horizontal asymptote is:
   $$y = \frac{\text{leading coefficient of } p(x)}{\text{leading coefficient of } q(x)}.$$
   3. If the degree of $p(x)$ › the degree of $q(x)$, there is no horizontal asymptote.

   3) **Oblique:** If the degree of $p(x)$ is exactly one more than the degree of $q(x)$, the slant asymptote is $y = p(x) \div q(x)$, using long division and ignoring the remainder.

They use it as I teach the section to find all the asymptotes. When doing the homework, I request they write the rules until they know them well in finding the asymptotes before graphing.

Nicki Feldman, *Pulaski Technical College*

■ ■ ■

Once again, interval notation is important here. Remind students that graphically, less than means lies below and greater than means lies above.

Bridgette L. Jacob, *Onondaga Community College*

■ ■ ■

4.5 Rational Functions

- Find the domain and graph a rational function, identifying all asymptotes.
- Solve applied problems involving rational functions.

Teaching Tips

I usually take a couple of class periods to cover this section since graphs of rational functions can vary so widely in appearance. Also, I stress the importance of using the calculator carefully when graphing rational functions because the TI-83/84 does not accurately display asymptotes. I stress the importance of finding and drawing any asymptotes first and then using the calculator's graph and table to help graph points.

Renée M. Macaluso, *Arizona Western College*

■ ■ ■

I challenge students to make a general sketch of the graph of a rational function based on their knowledge of horizontal and vertical asymptotes, *x*-intercepts, *y*-intercepts, and basic point plotting. Students then use the calculator to check their work.

Caroline Martinson, *Jefferson Community College*

■ ■ ■

Keeping calculus in mind (limits in particular), I begin by explaining the large-scale behavior of rational functions (horizontal asymptotes) followed by interior considerations (finding zeros and vertical asymptotes) and graphing these by hand.

Pavel Sikorskii, *Michigan State University*

4.6 Polynomial and Rational Inequalities

- Solve polynomial and rational inequalities.

Section 4.6

Polynomial inequalities are usually OK for students. For rational inequalities, students attempt to multiply through the inequality by the LCD. The problem with this method is remembering to include the critical values from the LCD when testing intervals.

Tim Chappell, *Penn Valley Community College*

■ ■ ■

Students have the most trouble deciding if the endpoints of the solution intervals for rational inequalities should be included (or not).

Caroline Martinson, *Jefferson Community College*

■ ■ ■

This section can be very frustrating to me because it seems as though the students often ignore the steps in solving these inequalities and make up their own rules. Thus far, I haven't come across the best way to emphasize that solving these inequalities is not like solving linear inequalities or quadratic equations. The best method for me is to give students a take-home quiz over the these sections.

Renée M. Macaluso, *Arizona Western College*

■ ■ ■

I would suggest making a connection to the previous two lectures and having students solve these using graphs. It is important to warn them not to cross multiply to solve rational inequalities.

Pavel Sikorskii, *Michigan State University*

Teaching Tips

Section 5.1

Explain that the inverse of a relation can be found by switching the x- and y- values. Develop this through sets of points to graphs and then to algebra.

Explain also that the inverse of a relation can be found by performing the opposite operations in opposite order. That is the only way to undo what the original function did. I use examples such as replacing a faulty part on a car.

Tim Chappell, *Penn Valley Community College*

■ ■ ■

Stress the fact that throughout their math lives, students have been taught how to do something, then they have been taught how to undo it. Nearly all operations or processes in math have an inverse operation or process that they also learn. That is what inverse functions are all about.

Luke Dowell, *Seward County Community College*

■ ■ ■

I write out step-by-step instructions for finding an inverse.

Steps for finding inverse
1. Replace $f(x)$ with y.
2. Trade or switch x and y.
3. Solve for y.
4. Replace y with f^{-1}, which is inverse notation.

This tends to cut down on the questions students have when trying to do these particular skills.

Nicki Feldman, *Pulaski Technical College*

■ ■ ■

Determining whether a function is one-to-one graphically does not seem to present a great problem for students but determining this from an equation is a bit more difficult for them. This is a good time to capitalize on what they have learned about the connections between the equation and the graph of a function.

Bridgette L. Jacob, *Onondaga Community College*

Objectives

5.1 Inverse Functions

- Determine whether a function is one-to-one, and if it is, find a formula for its inverse.
- Simplify expressions of the type $(f \circ f^{-1})(x)$ and $(f^{-1} \circ f)(x)$.

5.2 Exponential Functions and Graphs

- Graph exponential equations and functions.
- Solve applied problems involving exponential functions and their graphs.

Teaching Tips

Section 5.2

Be sure to develop e through compounding. Use a spreadsheet or graphing calculator with tables. This is a short section. I use Financial features on the TI graphing calculator for various auto loans, home loans, or investments. Students really get into it, and I assign a short paper over loans or investments.

Tim Chappell, *Penn Valley Community College*

■ ■ ■

I like to use tables to show the difference between polynomial functions and exponential functions as x gets larger.

Luke Dowell, *Seward County Community College*

■ ■ ■

This is a great section to answer the question, "When am I ever going to use this?" Not only do you show students the world applications, but you also can calm their phobia of word problems.

Nicki Feldman, *Pulaski Technical College*

■ ■ ■

Students' previous work with transformations will help them to recognize graphs of exponential functions and to sketch graphs of them. When working through the applied problems, the only method students have at this time to solve for the input value or exponent, some unit of time, is to graph the exponential function. Make sure to review this since they will need to determine the appropriate viewing window.

Bridgette L. Jacob, *Onondaga Community College*

■ ■ ■

I begin this section by having the students work out how much they would receive over a month's time from parents/boss/friend if they received 1¢ the first day, 2¢ the second, 4¢ the third, and so on. They are surprised at how quickly it grows at the end of the month and the power of exponential functions. We also discuss how exponential functions can be beneficial (as in investments) or harmful (as in credit card debt), depending on the situation.

Renée M. Macaluso, *Arizona Western College*

■ ■ ■

A short historical research project to find out about e is usually appreciated. This is often the first time students have ever heard of Euler or this number. When students realize that money (compound interest) and exponential functions are related, they begin to pay more attention.

Caroline Martinson, *Jefferson Community College*

■ ■ ■

I emphasize basic properties of exponential functions, show some graphs of transformed exponential functions, and do an example on the compound interest formula, which leads to an exponential equation that I solve graphically here.

Pavel Sikorskii, *Michigan State University*

Teaching Tips

Section 5.3

I have students convert between addition and subtraction, multiplication and division, and square roots and squares. Then I introduce logarithms and have them convert between logarithms and exponentials.

Earthquake magnitude and pH are two problem types I always cover.

Tim Chappell, *Penn Valley Community College*

■ ■ ■

Students usually need help remembering the basic properties of exponents. At the beginning of this section I review the following properties and leave them visible throughout the class.

1. $a^0 = 1$

2. $a^{-n} = \dfrac{1}{a^n}$

3. $a^{1/n} = \sqrt[n]{a}$

Nicki Feldman, *Pulaski Technical College*

■ ■ ■

Just the term logarithm sends some students running in the other direction! It is helpful beginning this chapter with inverse functions so students can immediately see the connection between exponential and logarithmic functions. Examining and discussing real-life scenarios that can be modeled by a logarithmic function may convince students of the importance of this family of functions.

Bridgette L. Jacob, *Onondaga Community College*

■ ■ ■

Just the word logarithm sends most students into a panic. I spend much time in class showing students what a logarithm is (the inverse of an exponential function) and why we write it the way we do. Also, we do many examples of just writing logs as exponential equations and vice versa and the students work some on their own in class, which they turn in, so that I can see if they understand it.

Renée M. Macaluso, *Arizona Western College*

■ ■ ■

From the moment that the definition of a logarithmic function is given, you will likely hear me shouting or whispering, "logs are exponents."

Caroline Martinson, *Jefferson Community College*

■ ■ ■

The definition is very important and plenty of examples should be done in class to make sure that students understand it.

Pavel Sikorskii, *Michigan State University*

5.3 Logarithmic Functions and Graphs

- Graph logarithmic functions.
- Find common and natural logarithms with and without a calculator.
- Convert between exponential and logarithmic equations.
- Change logarithm bases.

5.4 Properties of Logarithmic Functions

- Convert from logarithms of products, powers, and quotients to expressions in terms of individual logarithms, and conversely.

- Simplify expressions of the type $\log_a a^x$ and $a^{\log_a x}$.

Teaching Tips

Section 5.4

I tell my students that a logarithmic expression is essentially an exponent. I then develop the rules for logarithms from the rules for exponents.

Tim Chappell, *Penn Valley Community College*

■ ■ ■

Students can find the homework questions in this section confusing. After going over all of the properties, I make sure we do some sample problems from the exercises as a class before I turn them loose on the assignment.

Nicki Feldman, *Pulaski Technical College*

■ ■ ■

Students seem to be able to work with one logarithm property at a time; however, when asked to write two or more logarithms as a single logarithm, this causes some difficulty. Remind students to apply the power rule first and then the product and quotient rules from left to right.

Bridgette L. Jacob, *Onondaga Community College*

■ ■ ■

As long as students understand what a logarithm is from Section 5.3, they usually do well in this section.

Renée M. Macaluso, *Arizona Western College*

■ ■ ■

The product, quotient, and power rules are just restatements of rules the student already knows about exponents because "logs are exponents."

Caroline Martinson, *Jefferson Community College*

■ ■ ■

This is a skill and drill section where I try to do as many examples as I can to illustrate the properties. I also prove some of the properties using the exponential rules and warn students about some common mistakes (i.e., log of a sum is not equal to sum of logs, etc.).

Pavel Sikorskii, *Michigan State University*

Teaching Tips

Section 5.5

I focus on equations in this section that will be used in the applications in the next section.

Tim Chappell, *Penn Valley Community College*

■ ■ ■

This section usually warrants two days in our curriculum. I give students the following information:

To Solve Equations with Variables as Exponents

1. Try to make the bases the same and use: If $U^x = U^y$, then $x = y$.
2. If you can't make the bases the same, take the log of both sides then use $\log_a X^r = r\log_a X$.

To Solve Equations with Logs

1. If there is only one log in the problem, use the definition $\log_a x = y$ is equivalent to $a^y = x$.
   (If the log has a coefficient in front of it, move the coefficient back to an exponent before you use the definition.)
2. If there are two or more logs in the problem, you must use properties to write one or two logarithms.
   a. If you can write it as a single logarithm, use step 1 above.
   b. If you have two logs that equal each other, use: If $\log_a M = \log_a N$, then $M = N$.

This gives students a place to start if they get stuck so they will not come back to class empty-handed.

Nicki Feldman, *Pulaski Technical College*

■ ■ ■

Remind students that they can check solutions to exponential equations algebraically by substituting them into the original equations. This may require the use of the calculator or they can check graphically with the graphing calculator. This holds true for logarithmic equations as well, but the calculator is limited to base 10 and base e, so a change of base may be necessary.

Bridgette L. Jacob, *Onondaga Community College*

■ ■ ■

The main concept that I usually emphasize to students is that log and ln are function names, not variables. They often misunderstand this and try to "cancel" log and ln by dividing them out.

Renée M. Macaluso, *Arizona Western College*

■ ■ ■

Emphasize the different strategies used to solve equations algebraically when the unknown is in the exponent or when the equation already includes log(s). Use the calculator to check your work. I want students to realize the times when all the algebra they know still isn't enough to solve a problem. Then is a good time to let the calculator "solve" the problem.

Caroline Martinson, *Jefferson Community College*

5.6 Applications and Models: Growth and Decay; Compound Interest

- Solve applied problems involving exponential growth and decay.
- Find models involving exponential and logarithmic functions.

Teaching Tips

Section 5.6

We do most of the problems in this section. I give the students the option of using the doubling/half-life shortcut or working it out from the growth/decay equation.

Tim Chappell, *Penn Valley Community College*

■ ■ ■

When covering exponential and logarithmic equations, you have a real opportunity to explore current events and topics of general interest. Do a little investigating around the community and within your own class, and find out what the hot topics are: suburban sprawl (logistics model or population growth), earthquakes (logarithms), radioactive waste or landfills (exponential decay), value of stocks or collectibles (exponential growth), cost of textbooks (exponential growth), etc., then use these topics for examples in class.

Amy Del Medico, *Waubonsee Community College*

■ ■ ■

This section serves as a nice wrap-up to the chapter. Students may have difficulty writing the exponential equations from the information in the problems, so spend some class time demonstrating this procedure for them.

Bridgette L. Jacob, *Onondaga Community College*

■ ■ ■

This is a fun section because the students can see how useful exponential functions are in real applications. We complete many examples in this section.

Renée M. Macaluso, *Arizona Western College*

■ ■ ■

In this lecture, in addition to examples on exponential growth (population growth) and exponential decay (radioactive decay), I show students the annuity formulas (both future value and present value). Typically, I do an example on a retirement annuity and calculating a mortgage payment.

Pavel Sikorskii, *Michigan State University*

Teaching Tips

Section 6.1

What I have found to be very helpful to students is a chart with correlations between the system, lines, solutions, slopes, and equations.

Marc D. Campbell, *Daytona Beach Community College*

■ ■ ■

Most of my students are already familiar with solving a basic system of equations in two variables. We look quickly at graphical solutions, and then we dedicate the remaining time to applications. The exercise set has a good variety of applications to choose from.

Tim Chappell, *Penn Valley Community College*

■ ■ ■

This is a review section for our students. I find it another opportune time to work on word-problem phobia.

Nicki Feldman, *Pulaski Technical College*

Section 6.2

I cover Sections 6.2 and 6.3 together in two class sessions. In the first day, I do two examples of solving 3 x 3 systems, then I jump into Section 6.3 to show them the matrix representation.

Tim Chappell, *Penn Valley Community College*

■ ■ ■

I emphasize the pictures of the possible solutions shown in the text for a much-needed visual aid to this section.

Nicki Feldman, *Pulaski Technical College*

■ ■ ■

Some students get lost when there are more than two equations in the system. I name the equations *A*, *B*, and *C* and then write "Add equations *A* and *C* to eliminate *y*" so they can follow what we did in their notes. I always joke about naming the equations Alice, Betty, and Carol, but *A*, *B*, and *C* are easier to write.

Carol Lucas, *University of Central Oklahoma*

This section may confuse students if the logic is not presented very clearly. It's easy for anyone to lose track of what they are doing.

Renée M. Macaluso, *Arizona Western College*

Chapter 6

Systems of Equations and Matrices

Objectives

6.1 Systems of Equations in Two Variables

- Solve a system of two linear equations in two variables by graphing.
- Solve a system of two linear equations in two variables using the substitution and the elimination methods.
- Use systems of two linear equations to solve applied problems.

6.2 Systems of Equations in Three Variables

- Solve systems of linear equations in three variables.
- Use systems of three equations to solve applied problems.
- Model a situation using a quadratic function.

6.3 Matrices and Systems of Equations

- Solve systems of equations using matrices.

6.4 Matrix Operations

- Add, subtract, and multiply matrices when possible.
- Write a matrix equation equivalent to a system of equations.

6.5 Inverses of Matrices

- Find the inverse of a square matrix, if it exists.
- Use inverses of matrices to solve systems of equations.

Teaching Tips

Section 6.3

I use the second day to go over Gaussian elimination again. I teach students how to do reduced row echelon form (rref) on the TI, and I allow them to use the calculator to solve systems they have created for an application problem.

Due to the length of time that a 3 x 3 system takes, I sometimes give a one-question quiz over solving a 3 x 3 system. If they get the question completely right, then they don't have to work that problem on the test.

Tim Chappell, *Penn Valley Community College*

■ ■ ■

The students like this section, but I make them kill a lot of trees! I have them rewrite the matrix with explanations of how they are changing the matrix on every step. This makes it much easier to find mistakes along with keeping the students organized and focused as to the next step that will be taken.

Nicki Feldman, *Pulaski Technical College*

■ ■ ■

Students like matrices when they figure out that they can use them on their calculators to solve systems of equations, which can get really tedious when they're done by hand.

Renée M. Macaluso, *Arizona Western College*

■ ■ ■

Section 6.4

I use salary schedules and tax tables as examples of matrix multiplication.

Tim Chappell, *Penn Valley Community College*

■ ■ ■

This is an optional section for us to teach, but students like it. They see that the old way of doing these by hand is often faster than using the calculator and they can always check all work on their calculator.

Nicki Feldman, *Pulaski Technical College*

■ ■ ■

Section 6.5

I like to relate the method of inverse matrices to the method of solving a simple linear equation like $ax = b$. I find students can relate well to the concept of inverse matrices.

I don't like the shortcut approaches to finding inverses of 2 x 2 matrices, and since finding inverses of 3 x 3 matrices can be lengthy, I require students to set up the matrix equation on paper and to solve it using the graphing calculator.

Tim Chappell, *Penn Valley Community College*

■ ■ ■

I do one example of finding an inverse by hand. We do them on the calculators from then on.

Renée M. Macaluso, *Arizona Western College*

Teaching Tips

Section 6.6

Cramer's Rule is much more popular with students than Gauss-Jordan elimination. Using graphing calculators is also widely accepted.

Carol Lucas, *University of Central Oklahoma*

Section 6.7

This section is difficult to present thoroughly in one class session. Students quickly catch on to graphing a linear inequality in two variables. Much more time is spent on graphing systems of inequalities.

I usually avoid exercise sets that set up a part of the process. I prefer to jump in and work from beginning to end. I have found, though, that students need each of the preliminary exercises to prepare them for the multiple steps in linear programming.

Tim Chappell, *Penn Valley Community College*

■ ■ ■

This section can enlighten students as to why they ever had to learn systems of inequalities. If time permits, I like to have the students make their own word problem in a group, coming up with a company that will need to use linear programming.

Nicki Feldman, *Pulaski Technical College*

■ ■ ■

If I am running short on time, I skip linear programming, which I hate to do because the topic is one of my favorites. However, toward the end of the semester, we are often running out of time and students are getting tired.

Renée M. Macaluso, *Arizona Western College*

Section 6.8

When you discuss the topic, make sure to begin with simple fractions and illustrate how to add or subtract; then do the reverse process with the fractions. Next, discuss partial fractions with polynomials.

Joseph DeGuzman, *Riverside College-Norco Campus*

■ ■ ■

Since these procedures are long, a continual emphasis on the "big picture" is helpful to keep students on track.

Both methods presented for decomposing fractions presuppose a basic understanding that some students lack. For the first method, choosing values for x to solve for the variables, you may need to remind your class that the equation is true for all x and thus you can choose any value to substitute for x. You may wish to substitute several values for x before choosing a value that will eliminate one of the variables.

For the second method, it will not be obvious to some students that the coefficients of the corresponding terms (x^2-terms, x-terms, etc.) must be the same. You may wish to show several simpler equations in a parallel form to convince them of this fact. Also, this may be the first time students have seen variables (like A and B) serving as coefficients of x^2 and x. This concept may also require additional explanation and some simpler examples.

6.6 Determinants and Cramer's Rule

- Evaluate determinants of square matrices.
- Use Cramer's rule to solve systems of equations.

6.7 Systems of Inequalities and Linear Programming

- Graph linear inequalities.
- Graph systems of linear inequalities.
- Solve linear programming problems.

6.8 Partial Fractions

- Decompose rational expressions into partial fractions.

Chapter 7

Conic Sections

Objectives

7.1   The Parabola

- Given an equation of a parabola, complete the square, if necessary, and then find the vertex, the focus, and the directrix and graph the parabola.

7.2   The Circle and the Ellipse

- Given an equation of a circle, complete the square, if necessary, and then find the center and the radius and graph the circle.
- Given an equation of an ellipse, complete the square, if necessary, and then find the center, the vertices, and the foci and graph the ellipse.

Teaching Tips

Chapter 7

For the study of conics, I create a handout of all the formulas and I include things to look for when determining which conic section is represented by a particular equation.

Amy Del Medico, *Waubonsee Community College*

■ ■ ■

Many students will be interested in the geometric shapes formed by the intersection of a plane with a cone. You may wish to ask whether a line and a point are also conic sections, and how they are formed.

Section 7.1

Although the algebra is essential, the connections make the material meaningful—satellite dish, spotlight, microphone.

Caroline Martinson, *Jefferson Community College*

■ ■ ■

Let students use the definition "the set of all points in a plane equidistant from a fixed line and a fixed point not on the line" to draw such a set of points. You can provide a list of graphs like "line, circle, parabola, ellipse" and see if they can choose the correct shape. Students may need to know that the distance of a point to a line is the perpendicular distance to that line.

Up to this point, most students have not encountered a situation where they choose a coordinate system; that has always been a "given." This would be a good place to explain that when modeling a problem, the coordinate system is chosen to make the solution as easy as possible.

Section 7.2

Although the algebra is essential, the connections make the material meaningful—medical procedure, whispering gallery, orbits.

Caroline Martinson, *Jefferson Community College*

■ ■ ■

Let students use the definitions "the set of all points in a plane that are at a fixed distance from a fixed point in the plane" and "the set of all points in a plane, the sum of whose distances from two fixed points is constant" to draw such a set of points. You can provide a list of graphs like "line, circle, parabola, ellipse" and see if they can choose the correct shape. Both of these graphs can be drawn with pencil, tacks, and string.

Point out the difference between the equation of a circle and the equation of an ellipse by emphasizing the coefficients of the x^2- and y^2-terms.

Teaching Tips

Section 7.3

Although the algebra is essential, the connections make the material meaningful—navigation, cooling tower, path of a comet.

Caroline Martinson, *Jefferson Community College*

■ ■ ■

Let students use the definition "the set of all points in a plane for which the absolute value of the difference of the distances from two fixed points is constant" to draw such a set of points. You can provide a list of graphs like "line, circle, parabola, ellipse, hyperbola" and see if they can choose the correct shape. This is the most difficult definition in this chapter to visualize this way.

If students are having difficulty knowing which axis contains the vertices, point out that for an equation like $\dfrac{x^2}{a^2} - \dfrac{y^2}{b^2} = 1$, when $x = 0$ (on the y-axis), there is no solution to $-\dfrac{y^2}{b^2} = 1$.

Section 7.4

Before one of these problems is attempted, try to have the students identify the lines and conic sections. Then have them decide how many solutions they should come up with. It really reinforces conic sections.

Nicki Feldman, *Pulaski Technical College*

■ ■ ■

Many students will find one solution to a system and quit. Emphasize that many of these systems have more than one solution, and all of them must be found to "solve" the system of equations. You may wish to step carefully through an example like Example 3, where the equations $x = \pm\sqrt{2}$ and $y = \pm\sqrt{7}$ yield four distinct solutions to the system of equations.

7.3 The Hyperbola

- Given an equation of a hyperbola, complete the square, if necessary, and then find the center, the vertices, and the foci and graph the hyperbola.

7.4 Nonlinear Systems of Equations

- Solve a nonlinear system of equations.
- Use nonlinear systems of equations to solve applied problems.
- Graph nonlinear systems of inequalities.

Chapter 8
Sequences, Series, and Combinatorics

Objectives

8.1 Sequences and Series

- Find terms of sequences given the nth term.
- Look for a pattern in a sequence and try to determine a general term.
- Convert between sigma notation and other notation for a series.
- Construct the terms of a recursively defined sequence.

8.2 Arithmetic Sequences and Series

- For any arithmetic sequence, find the nth term when n is given and n when the nth term is given, and given two terms, find the common difference and construct the sequence.
- Find the sum of the first n terms of an arithmetic sequence.

Teaching Tips

Section 8.1

Finding the terms of a sequence or calculating a sum does not seem to give students much trouble. However, students may have difficulty writing the general term of a sequence and/or representing a sum with sigma notation.

Bridgette L. Jacob, *Onondaga Community College*

■ ■ ■

The most difficult part of this section is getting students used to the notation and finding general formulas for the terms of the sequences. I emphasize to the students that it takes a lot of practice.

Renée M. Macaluso, *Arizona Western College*

■ ■ ■

I emphasize finding the nth term, sigma notation, and recursively defined sequences. (The Fibonacci sequence is a nice example to use.)

Pavel Sikorskii, *Michigan State University*

Section 8.2

I think it is important to guide students to discover the formula for the nth term of a sequence by writing a sequence in such a way that the pattern emerges. I also share with them the story of Gauss when we do the arithmetic series sum formula.

Carol Lucas, *University of Central Oklahoma*

■ ■ ■

Students are often interested in learning how to sum a long sequence of numbers by using a formula. I begin by having them sum the numbers 1–10 and then using the formula to demonstrate that it really does work. Next, I have them sum every odd number to 201.

Sharon Testone, *Onondaga Community College*

Teaching Tips

Section 8.3

I use the same strategy here for finding the formula for the nth term of a geometric sequence that I use with the arithmetic sequences.

Infinite geometric sequences usually cannot be covered on the same day as the rest of the section because of time constraints.

When testing this material, I write the formulas in random order on the blackboard. I thought students were missing problems because they didn't know the formulas, but they actually didn't know which formula to use. I then realized that more practice was needed where the different types of sequence and series problems were mixed together.

Carol Lucas, *University of Central Oklahoma*

■ ■ ■

It is very interesting to students that an infinite series can have a finite sum. This concept is especially difficult before they enter calculus but can get them interested in starting calculus the next semester.

Renée M. Macaluso, *Arizona Western College*

■ ■ ■

Here, the emphasis should be on geometric series and where they converge.

Pavel Sikorskii, *Michigan State University*

Section 8.4

Mathematical induction has tremendous importance in computer science. Use several examples involving pattern recognition to introduce this topic.

James Ball, *Indiana State University*

■ ■ ■

Mathematical Induction is one of the most difficult topics for students to understand. Be sure that they clearly list S_n, S_1, S_k, and S_{k+1}. Many of the students may have completed deductive proofs in a geometry course, but often they have never used proof by induction. They will need much guidance in this section.

Sharon Testone, *Onondaga Community College*

8.3 Geometric Sequences and Series

- Identify the common ratio of a geometric sequence, and find a given term and the sum of the first n terms.
- Find the sum of an infinite geometric series, if it exists.

8.4 Mathematical Induction

- List the statements of an infinite sequence that is defined by a formula.
- Do proofs by mathematical induction.

8.5 Combinatorics: Permutations

- Evaluate factorial and permutation notation and solve related applied problems.

8.6 Combinatorics: Combinations

- Evaluate combination notation and solve related applied problems.

8.7 The Binomial Theorem

- Expand a power of a binomial using Pascal's triangle or factorial notation.
- Find a specific term of a binomial expansion.
- Find the total number of subsets of a set of n objects.

8.8 Probability

- Compute the probability of a simple event.

Teaching Tips

Section 8.5

Individually, Sections 8.5 and 8.6 are not difficult. However, when problems are not in the context of the section, students often have difficulty deciding whether to use a permutation or a combination. It helps to do a sheet of mixed problems after covering Section 8.6 that the students can work on together and turn in.

Renée M. Macaluso, *Arizona Western College*

Section 8.6

Students have problems determining the difference between permutations and combinations. I have the students think about the "co" in combinations and relate it to "co-captains." Having co-captains of Harry and Joe is the same as having co-captains of Joe and Harry; thus order does not matter. If order does matter, then we would have a permutation (i.e., President and Vice-President).

Sharon Testone, *Onondaga Community College*

Section 8.7

Some students will prefer to use Pascal's Triangle to find the coefficients of a binomial expansion while others will choose to use combinations. There may be a student or two who needs to write out the entire binomial expansion to find a specific term. As long as they can do both, expand a binomial and find a specific term, mission accomplished.

Bridgette L. Jacob, *Onondaga Community College*

■ ■ ■

Was the triangle really Pascal's? Time for another historical moment, or research project.

Caroline Martinson, *Jefferson Community College*

Section 8.8

Students often find this chapter very interesting because it can be related to real-world examples. I always begin the section by asking my students to list several places where they have seen probability used. I then show a simple example of a coin toss.

Sharon Testone, *Onondaga Community College*

AVAILABLE SUPPLEMENTS

Student Supplements	Instructor Supplements

Student Supplements

Graphing Calculator Manual
ISBN: 0-321-52908-1, 978-0-321-52908-4
• By Judith A. Penna
• Contains keystroke level instruction for the Texas Instruments TI-83 Plus, TI-84 Plus, and TI-89
• Teaches students how to use a graphing calculator using actual examples and exercises from the main text
• Mirrors the topic order to the main text to provide a just-in-time mode of instruction
• Automatically ships with each new copy of the text

Student's Solutions Manual
ISBN: 0-321-52904-9, 978-0-321-52904-6
• By Judith A. Penna
• Contains completely worked-out solutions with step-by-step annotations for all odd-numbered exercises in the exercise sets, with the exception of the Collaborative Discussion and Writing exercises, and for all the odd-numbered review exercises and all chapter test exercises

Video Lectures on CD with Optional Captioning
ISBN: 0-321-52910-3, 978-0-321-52910-7
• Complete set of digitized videos on CD-ROM for student use at home or on campus
• Ideal for distance learning or supplemental instruction
• Features authors Judy Beecher and Judy Penna working through and explaining key examples from the text

Instructor Supplements

Annotated Instructor's Edition
ISBN: 0-321-53191-4, 978-0-321-53191-9
• Includes all answers to the exercise sets, usually right on the page where the exercises appear
• Readily accessible answers help both new and experienced instructors prepare for class efficiently

NEW! Insider's Guide
ISBN: 0-321-52912-X, 978-0-321-52912-1
• Includes resources to help faculty with course preparation and classroom management
• Provides helpful teaching tips, conversion guide, and a sample syllabus
• Includes black-line masters of grids and number lines for transparency masters or test preparation

Instructor's Solutions Manual
ISBN: 0-321-52893-X, 978-0-321-52893-3
• By Judith A. Penna
• Contains worked-out solutions to all exercises in the exercise sets, including the Collaborative Discussion and Writing exercises, and solutions for all end-of-chapter material

Printed Test Bank
ISBN: 0-321-52894-8, 978-0-321-52894-0
• By Laurie Hurley
• Contains four free-response test forms for each chapter following the same format and having the same level of difficulty as the tests in the main text, plus two multiple-choice test forms for each chapter
• Provides six forms of the final examination, four with free-response questions and two with multiple-choice questions

Pearson Adjunct Support Center
• Offers consultation on suggested syllabi, helpful tips for using the textbook support package, assistance with content, and advice on classroom strategies
• Available Sunday through Thursday evenings from 5 P.M. to midnight, Eastern
• e-mail: AdjunctSupport@aw.com; Telephone: 1-800-435-4084; fax: 1-877-262-9774

ADDITIONAL SUPPLEMENTS

TestGen®

TestGen enables instructors to build, edit, print, and administer tests using a computerized bank of questions developed to cover all the objectives of the text. TestGen is algorithmically based, allowing instructors to create multiple but equivalent versions of the same question or test with the click of a button. Instructors can also modify test bank questions or add new questions. Tests can be printed or administered online. The software and testbank are available for download from www.aw-bc.com/irc.

PowerPoint® Lecture Presentation and Active Learning Questions

The PowerPoint Lecture slides feature presentations written and designed specifically for this text, including figures and examples from the text. The Active Learning Questions, prepared in PowerPoint, are intended for use with classroom response systems and include multiple choice questions to review lecture material. The PowerPoint Lecture Presentation and Active Learning Questions are available for download from within MyMathLab and from www.aw-bc.com/irc.

MathXL® Tutorials on CD

ISBN: 0-321-52913-8, 978-0-321-52913-8

This interactive tutorial CD-ROM provides algorithmically generated practice exercises that are correlated at the objective level to the exercises in the textbook. Every practice exercise is accompanied by an example and a guided solution designed to involve students in the solution process. Selected exercises may also include a video clip to help students visualize concepts. The software provides helpful feedback for incorrect answers and can generate printed summaries of students' progress.

InterAct Math Tutorial Website® www.interactmath.com

Get practice and tutorial help online! This interactive tutorial website provides algorithmically generated practice exercises that correlate directly to the exercises in the textbook. Students can retry an exercise as many times as they like with new values each time for unlimited practice and mastery. Every exercise is accompanied by an interactive guided solution that provides helpful feedback for incorrect answers, and students can also view a worked-out sample problem that steps them through an exercise similar to the one they're working on.

MathXL® Online Course

MathXL® is a powerful online homework, tutorial, and assessment system that uses algorithmically generated exercises correlated at the objective level to your textbook. Instructors can create and assign online homework and tests and can track students' results in MathXL's flexible online gradebook. Students can retry interactive tutorial exercises as many times as they like, with new values each time, for unlimited practice and mastery. They also receive a personalized study plan based on their test results that links directly to exercises for the objectives they need to study and retest. For more information, see page 55.

MyMathLab® Online Course

MyMathLab is a complete online course that offers all the features of MathXL plus a complete multimedia eBook, additional course-management features, and access to the Pearson Tutor Center. Powered by CourseCompass™ (Pearson's online teaching and learning environment) and by MathXL (our online homework, tutorial, and assessment system), MyMathLab makes it easy to deliver all or a portion of your course online. Instructors can easily customize MyMathLab to suit their students' needs and help increase their comprehension and success. For more information, see page 56.

Getting Started with MathXL®

Overview

MathXL® is a powerful online homework, tutorial, and assessment system tied to Pearson Addison-Wesley and Pearson Prentice Hall textbooks in Mathematics and Statistics. Ideal for use in a lecture, self-paced, or distance-learning course, MathXL diagnoses students' weaknesses and creates a personalized study plan based on their test results. MathXL provides students with unlimited practice using a database of algorithmically generated exercises correlated to the exercises in their textbook. Each tutorial exercise is accompanied by an interactive guided solution and a sample problem to help students improve their skills independently. Instructors can use MathXL to create online homework assignments, quizzes, and tests that are automatically graded and tracked. Instructors can view and manage all students' homework and test results, study plans, and tutorial work in MathXL's flexible online gradebook.

How to Adopt MathXL

1. **Getting Access**

   If you are interested in using MathXL for one or more of your courses, contact your Addison-Wesley sales representative to request a *MathXL Instructor Access Kit*. (If you are not sure who your sales representative is, go to www.aw-bc.com/replocator.) The access kit provides you with an **instructor access code** for registration.

2. **Registering**

   Registering is an easy process that takes only a few minutes, and you need to register only once, even if you are teaching more than one course with MathXL. Detailed instructions are included in the instructor access kit. As part of the registration process, you select a login name and password that you will use from then on to access your MathXL course. Once you have your instructor access code, go to www.mathxl.com, click the **Register** button, and follow the on-screen instructions to register and log in.

3. **Creating Your MathXL Course**

   Once you've registered, creating your MathXL course is easy! Simply log in at www.mathxl.com, go to the Course Manager, and click Create Course. You will be asked to select the textbook you are using and enter some very basic information about your course. You can create as many courses as you need, and you can customize course coverage to match your syllabus if you wish.

4. **Ordering Books for Your Students**

   To access your MathXL course, each student needs to register in MathXL using a student access code. The easiest way to supply your students with access codes is to order your textbook packaged with the *MathXL Student Access Kit*. Visit the **Books with MathXL** section of the website at www.mathxl.com for a complete list of package ISBNs.

How to Learn More about MathXL

- To learn more about MathXL, visit our website at www.mathxl.com, or contact your Addison-Wesley sales representative to schedule a demonstration.
- For detailed instructions on how to register, log in, and set up your first MathXL course, view or print the *Getting Started with MathXL* instructor guide from the **Support** section of the MathXL website at www.mathxl.com.

Getting Started with MyMathLab®

Overview

Powered by CourseCompass™ and MathXL®, MyMathLab is a series of text-specific online courses that accompany Pearson Addison-Wesley and Pearson Prentice Hall textbooks in Mathematics and Statistics. Since 2001, more than one million students at over 1100 colleges and universities have had more success in Math with MyMathLab's dependable and easy-to-use online homework, guided solutions, multimedia, tests, and eBooks. Pearson's premier, proven service teams provide training and support when you need it. And MyMathLab offers the broadest range of titles available for adoption.

When you adopt the MyMathLab course for your textbook, your students can view the textbook pages in electronic form and link to supplemental multimedia resources—such as animations and video clips—directly from the eBook. MyMathLab provides students with algorithmically generated tutorial exercises correlated to the exercises in their text, and the system generates individualized study plans based on student test results. MyMathLab's powerful homework and test managers and flexible online gradebook make it easy for instructors to create and manage online assignments that are automatically graded, so they can spend less time grading and more time teaching!

How to Adopt MyMathLab

1. Getting Access

If you are interested in using MyMathLab for one or more of your courses, you will need an **instructor access code**. You can receive an instructor access code in one of two ways:
- Request a *MyMathLab Instructor Access Kit* from your Addison-Wesley sales representative. To identify your sales representative, go to www.aw-bc.com/replocator.
- Request an access code online by visiting the **Getting Started** section of the MyMathLab website at www.mymathlab.com.

2. Registering

MyMathLab courses are accessed through an online learning environment called CourseCompass, so to adopt a MyMathLab course, you need to register in CourseCompass. Registering is an easy process that takes only a few minutes, and you need to register only once, even if you are teaching more than one MyMathLab course. As part of the registration process, you select a login name and password that you will use from then on to access your MyMathLab course. Once you have your instructor access code, go to www.coursecompass.com, click the **Register** button for instructors, and follow the on-screen instructions to register and log in.

3. Creating Your MyMathLab Course

Once you've registered in CourseCompass, creating your MyMathLab course is easy! You will simply be asked to select the course materials for your textbook and enter some very basic information about your course. Approximately one business day later (and often after only an hour or two), you will be notified via e-mail that your course is ready, and you will then be able to log in and begin exploring MyMathLab.

4. Ordering Books for Your Students

To access your MyMathLab course, each student needs to register in CourseCompass using a student access code. The easiest way to supply your students with access codes is to order your textbook packaged with the *MyMathLab Student Access Kit*. Visit the **Books with MyMathLab** section of the website at www.mymathlab.com for a complete list of package ISBNs.

How to Learn More about MyMathLab

- To learn more about MyMathLab, visit our website at www.mymathlab.com, or contact your Addison-Wesley sales representative to schedule a demonstration.
- For detailed instructions on how to register, log in, and set up your first MyMathLab course, view or print the *Getting Started with MyMathLab* and *CourseCompass* instructor guide from the **Support** section of the MyMathLab website at www.mymathlab.com.

HELPFUL TIPS FOR USING SUPPLEMENTS AND TECHNOLOGY

Marc D. Campbell, *Daytona Beach Community College*

- Our math department uses MyMathLab, the digital videos, MathXL, and TestGen on a daily basis. MyMathLab is the main source of delivery in the online class we offer in the math department. It is also an integral part of our computerized instruction course. The digital videos are used in our half-and-half courses. MathXL is a valuable tool which is housed in the Learning Center, a place where students can receive additional help in understanding concepts. We use TestGen to make common tests to ensure consistency throughout the department.

Tim Chappell, *Penn Valley Community College*

- We encourage our students to take advantage of MyMathLab. There is a link on our class homepage with the directions on how to log in. We don't require participation in MyMathLab, but students frequently mention the help the video clips and tutorials provide.

- I used TestGen the first year we used the book, but I create my own tests from scratch now. I encourage its use for someone teaching the course for the first time.

Amy Del Medico, *Waubonsee Community College*

- I like to use TestGen not only to create my exams, but also to provide students with practice exams. It's easy to do since you can have the program algorithmically change the numerical values in each problem. I also like this feature to create several versions of the same exam when I have a full class and students are sitting close together during exams.

- A full set of videos that accompany the textbook are made available to students through our library. If a student needs to review a particular topic, if a student was absent, or if a student needs an alternate explanation of a topic, he/she has access to the videos outside of the classroom.

- I include a link to the textbook's online resources on my Web page and encourage students to use this for extra help. The problems with hints encourage students to ask themselves the "leading" type of questions that instructors use in class.

Luke Dowell, *Seward County Community College*

- I have used TestGen to make up review sheets. It took a while to get used to, but after that it worked well. I write my own tests, so I do not use it for regular exams.

Nicki Feldman, *Pulaski Technical College*

- We require all students to buy the accompanying graphing calculator support manual. It shows the keystrokes for the examples from the text in a step-by-step process. It is also great for the students taking online or distance learning.

- The videos are made available to all students in our library. We also make them available in our math labs. They are a great place to start if a student misses a particular lecture or needs additional help with a specific concept.

- We have moved to using Math XL with our online students. The tutorials are great and the students can work unlimited problems regenerated by the program until a concept is mastered.

Bridgette L. Jacob, *Onondaga Community College*

■ I currently teach this precalculus course online, so my students use MyMathLab extensively with great success. It provides nice flexibility for different types of learners. Many of them find the videos very helpful, especially without the traditional classroom setting. They also find the *Help Me Solve* feature of the homework very helpful.

■ In the traditional classroom, again MyMathLab provides much flexibility, especially when completing the homework. Students can use MyMathLab exclusively or as a supplement to textbook problems.

Renée M. Macaluso, *Arizona Western College*

■ We use MyMathLab in our online college algebra and precalculus classes. I don't teach the classes online so I don't use MyMathLab with this textbook. If I have to cancel class and it won't be easy to make up the material, I will have someone show the students a video over a section.

Caroline Martinson, *Jefferson Community College*

■ For online students (completely asynchronous) the videos are the resource the auditory learners need. Many online students have told me they couldn't have been successful in the course without this audio/video resource. For the students who take this class face-to-face, the videos are also an excellent resource. We have VHS tapes in the math learning lab and also in the library for students to use on campus and at home. Some students find the videos so helpful they purchase the Digital Video Tutor (CDs) for their personal use.

■ I don't have graduate teaching assistants at the community college. MathXL has become my staff of GTAs. I consider MathXL an essential tool to increase student learning. I give all students a "Guide to MathXL." It is much more appreciated by the online students than the on-campus students. It is a one-page step-by-step of how to get started in MathXL. Answers to questions from prior semesters get added to this ever-evolving resource. I assign homework and quizzes using MathXL. I encourage students to use practice tests on MathXL and follow the personal study plan generated as a way to study for tests. If the classroom has Internet access, I will log in to MathXL for "sample" problems. During the first two weeks of the semester, I schedule one class meeting in a campus computer lab. Online students have found MathXL to be user-friendly. Many students have said that MathXL is a valuable supplement to the textbook and videos.

CONVERSION GUIDE

College Algebra: Graphs & Models, 4e

This conversion guide is designed to help you adapt your syllabus for Bittinger/Beecher/Ellenbogen/Penna's *College Algebra: Graphs & Models*, Third Edition to Bittinger/Beecher/Ellenbogen/Penna's *College Algebra: Graphs & Models*, Fourth Edition by providing a section-by-section cross reference between the third and fourth editions. Additional revisions and refinements have been made in addition to the changes specified here.

College Algebra: Graphs & Models, 4e		College Algebra: Graphs & Models, 3e	
R	**Basic Concepts of Algebra**	**R**	**Basic Concepts of Algebra**
R.1	The Real-Number System	R.1	The Real-Number System
R.2	Integer Exponents, Scientific Notation, and Order of Operations	R.2	Integer Exponents, Scientific Notation, and Order of Operations
R.3	Addition, Subtraction, and Multiplication of Polynomials	R.3	Addition, Subtraction, and Multiplication of Polynomials
R.4	Factoring	R.4	Factoring
R.5	The Basics of Equation Solving	R.7	The Basics of Equation Solving
R.6	Rational Expressions	R.5	Rational Expressions
R.7	Radical Notation and Rational Exponents	R.6	Radical Notation and Rational Exponents
1	**Graphs, Functions, and Models**	**Formed from Chapters 1 and 2 of Third Edition**	
1.1	Introduction to Graphing	1.1	Introduction to Graphing
1.2	Functions and Graphs	1.2	Functions and Graphs
1.3	Linear Functions, Slope, and Applications	1.3	Linear Functions, Slope, and Applications
1.4	Equations of Lines and Modeling	1.4	Equations of Lines and Modeling
1.5	Linear Equations, Functions, Zeros, and Models	2.1	Linear Equations, Functions, and Models
1.6	Solving Linear Inequalities	2.6	Solving Linear Inequalities (partial)
2	**More on Functions**	**Formed from Chapters 1 and 3 of Third Edition**	
2.1	Increasing, Decreasing, and Piecewise Functions	1.5	More on Functions
2.2	The Algebra of Functions	1.6	The Algebra of Functions (partial)
2.3	The Composition of Functions	1.6	The Algebra of Functions (partial)
2.4	Symmetry and Transformations	1.7	Symmetry and Transformations
2.5	Variation and Applications	3.7	Variation and Applications
3	**Quadratic Functions and Equations; Inequalities**	**Formed from material in Chapter 2 of Third Edition**	
3.1	The Complex Numbers	2.2	The Complex Numbers
3.2	Quadratic Equations, Functions, Zeros, and Models	2.3	Quadratic Equations, Functions, and Models
3.3	Analyzing Graphs of Quadratic Functions	2.4	Analyzing Graphs of Quadratic Functions

3.4	Solving Rational Equations and Radical Equations	2.5	More Equation Solving (partial)	
3.5	Solving Equations and Inequalities with Absolute Value	2.5	More Equation Solving (partial) and	
		2.6	Solving Linear Inequalities (partial)	

4 Polynomial and Rational Functions   **3 Polynomial and Rational Functions**

4.1	Polynomial Functions and Modeling	3.1	Polynomial Functions and Modeling
4.2	Graphing Polynomial Functions	3.2	Graphing Polynomial Functions
4.3	Polynomial Division; The Remainder and Factor Theorems	3.3	Polynomial Division; The Remainder and Factor Theorems
4.4	Theorems about Zeros of Polynomial Functions	3.4	Theorems about Zeros of Polynomial Functions
4.5	Rational Functions	3.5	Rational Functions
4.6	Polynomial and Rational Inequalities	3.6	Polynomial and Rational Inequalities

5 Exponential and Logarithmic Functions   **4 Exponential and Logarithmic Functions**

5.1	Inverse Functions	4.1	Inverse Functions
5.2	Exponential Functions and Graphs	4.2	Exponential Functions and Graphs
5.3	Logarithmic Functions and Graphs	4.3	Logarithmic Functions and Graphs
5.4	Properties of Logarithmic Functions	4.4	Properties of Logarithmic Functions
5.5	Solving Exponential and Logarithmic Equations	4.5	Solving Exponential and Logarithmic Equations
5.6	Applications and Models: Growth and Decay; Compound Interest	4.6	Applications and Models: Growth and Decay, and Compound Interest

6 Systems of Equations and Matrices   **5 Systems of Equations and Matrices**

6.1	Systems of Equations in Two Variables	5.1	Systems of Equations in Two Variables
6.2	Systems of Equations in Three Variables	5.2	Systems of Equations in Three Variables
6.3	Matrices and Systems of Equations	5.3	Matrices and Systems of Equations
6.4	Matrix Operations	5.4	Matrix Operations
6.5	Inverses of Matrices	5.5	Inverses of Matrices
6.6	Determinants and Cramer's Rule	5.6	Determinants and Cramer's Rule
6.7	Systems of Inequalities and Linear Programming	5.7	Systems of Inequalities and Linear Programming
6.8	Partial Fractions	5.8	Partial Fractions

7 Conic Sections   **6 Conic Sections**

7.1	The Parabola	6.1	The Parabola
7.2	The Circle and the Ellipse	6.2	The Circle and the Ellipse
7.3	The Hyperbola	6.3	The Hyperbola
7.4	Nonlinear Systems of Equations and Inequalities	6.4	Nonlinear Systems of Equations and Inequalities

8 Sequences, Series, and Combinatorics   **7 Sequences, Series, and Combinatorics**

8.1	Sequences and Series	7.1	Sequences and Series
8.2	Arithmetic Sequences and Series	7.2	Arithmetic Sequences and Series
8.3	Geometric Sequences and Series	7.3	Geometric Sequences and Series
8.4	Mathematical Induction	7.4	Mathematical Induction
8.5	Combinatorics: Permutations	7.5	Combinatorics: Permutations
8.6	Combinatorics: Combinations	7.6	Combinatorics: Combinations
8.7	The Binomial Theorem	7.7	The Binomial Theorem
8.8	Probability	7.8	Probability

Appendix: Basic Concepts from Geometry   **Appendix: Basic Concepts from Geometry**

USEFUL CLASSROOM RESOURCES FOR TEACHERS

Provided by:

Renée M. Macaluso, *Arizona Western College*

Review Worksheet   Name:

1) (R.1) For the following inequalities, graph them and write them in interval notation:
    a) $5 < x \le 8$
    b) $x \le -1$

2) (R.2) Simplify:
    a) 5^2
    b) 5^{-2}
    c) -5^2
    d) 5^0
    e) $(x^2y^{-3})^{-4}$
    f) $\dfrac{x^{-2}y}{x^{-7}y^3}$

3) (R.3) Multiply:
    a) $(x - 7)(x + 9)$
    b) $(x + 8)(x^2 - 2x + 4)$

4) (R.4) Factor:
    a) $x^2 - 9$
    b) $6x^2 - 7x - 5$
    c) $18xy + 12x^2$

5) (R.5) Solve for x:
    a) $3(x - 8) + 2 = 5x + 12$
    b) $x^2 + 5x = -6$

6) (R.6) Simplify:
    a) $\dfrac{x^2 - 4}{x^2 + 4x + 4}$
    b) $\dfrac{5}{x - 2} - \dfrac{x}{x + 3}$

7) (R.7) Simplify:
    a) $\sqrt{20}$
    b) $\sqrt{x^2}$
    c) $16^{3/2}$

Solutions to Review Worksheet

1) (R.1) For the following inequalities, graph them and write them in interval notation:
   a) $5 < x \le 8$
      $(5, 8]$
   b) $x \le -1$
      $(-?, -1]$

2) (R.2) Simplify:
   a) $5^2 = 25$
   b) $5^{-2} = 1/25$
   c) $-5^2 = -25$
   d) $5^0 = 1$
   e) $(x^2 y^{-3})^{-4} = x^{-8} y^{12}$
   f) $\dfrac{x^{-2} y}{x^{-7} y^3} = x^5 y^{-2}$

3) (R.3) Multiply:
   a) $(x - 7)(x + 9) = x^2 + 2x - 63$
   b) $(x + 8)(x^2 - 2x + 4) = x^3 + 6x^2 - 12x + 32$

4) (R.4) Factor:
   a) $x^2 - 9 = (x + 3)(x - 3)$
   b) $6x^2 - 7x - 5 = (2x + 1)(3x - 5)$
   c) $18xy + 12x^2 = 6x(3y + 4x)$

5) (R.5) Solve for x:
   a) $3(x - 8) + 2 = 5x + 12$
      $x = -17$
   b) $x^2 + 5x = -6$
      $x = -3, -2$

6) (R.6) Simplify:
   a) $\dfrac{x^2 - 4}{x^2 + 4x + 4} = \dfrac{x - 2}{x + 2}$
   b) $\dfrac{5}{x - 2} - \dfrac{x}{x + 3} = \dfrac{-x^2 + 7x + 15}{(x - 2)(x + 3)}$

7) (R.7) Simplify:
   a) $\sqrt{20} = 2\sqrt{5}$
   b) $\sqrt{x^2} = |x|$
   c) $16^{3/2} = 64$

TRANSPARENCY MASTERS AND TEST AIDS

TEST AID: NUMBER LINES

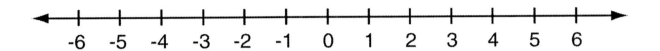

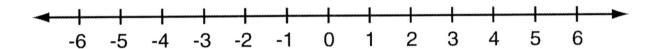

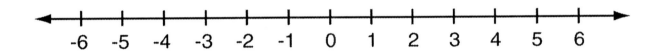

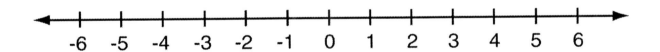

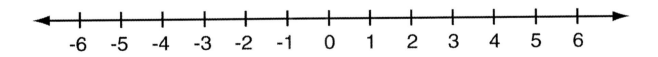

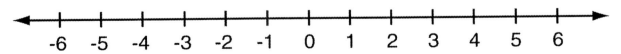

TEST AID: RECTANGULAR COORDINATE GRIDS

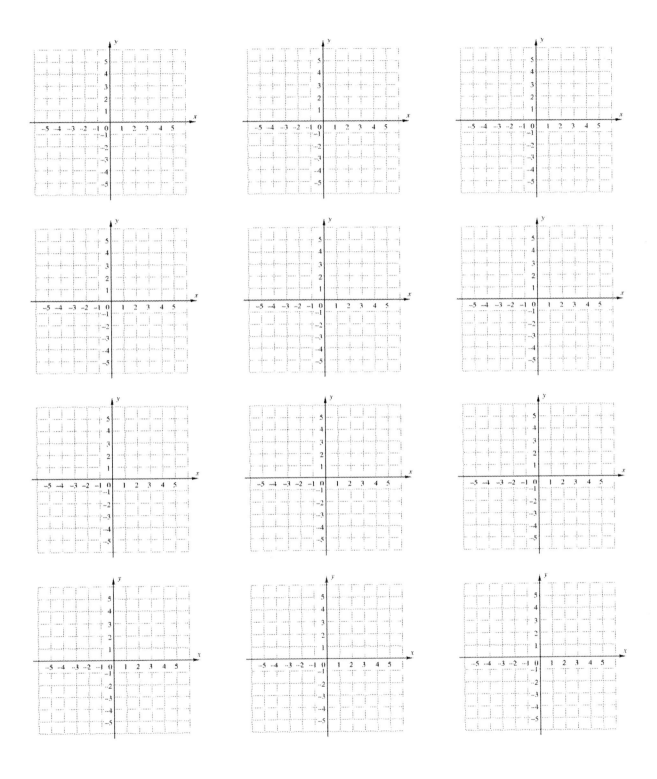

TEST AID: RECTANGULAR COORDINATE GRIDS

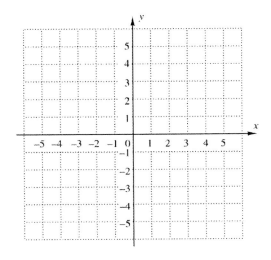

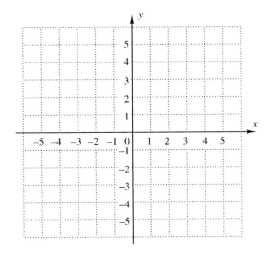

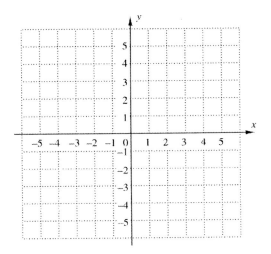

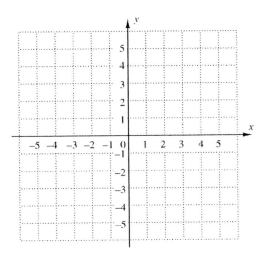

TRANSPARENCY MASTER: NUMBER LINES

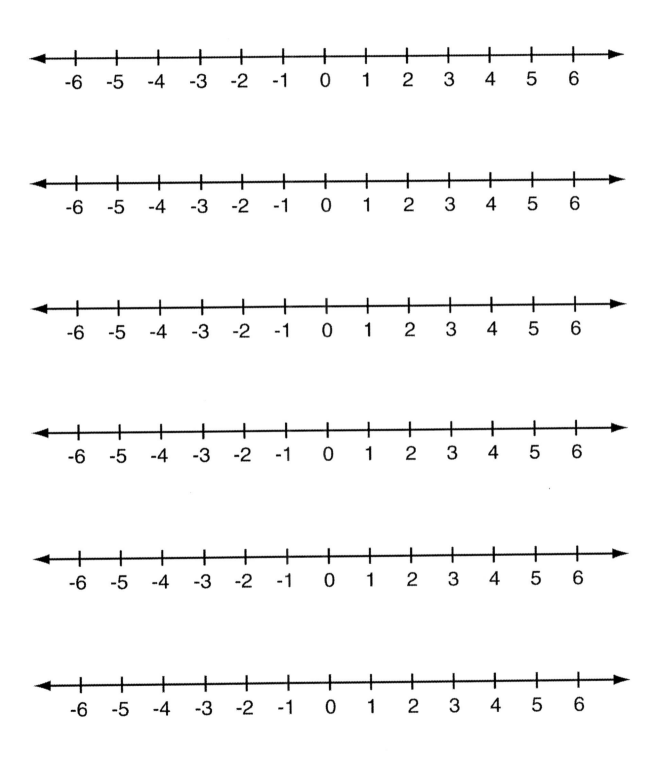

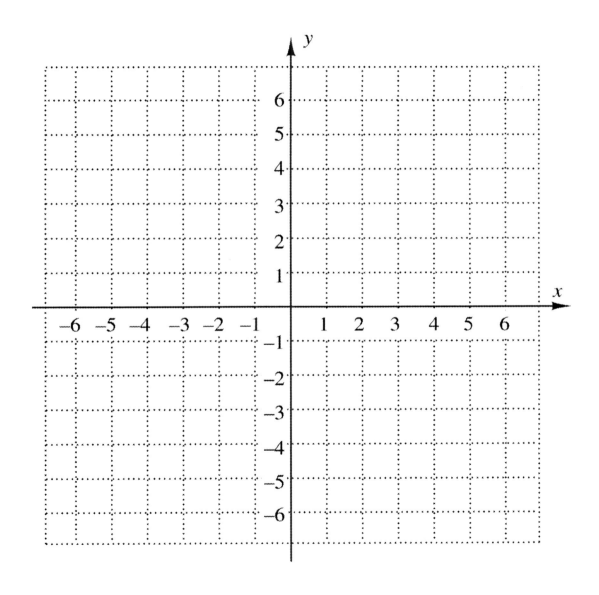

PROFESSIONAL BIBLIOGRAPHY

Davidson, Randy, and Ellen Levitov, *Overcoming Math Anxiety*, 2nd ed., Boston: Addison-Wesley/Longman, 2000.

Eggleton, Patrick, "Experiencing Radians," *Mathematics Teacher*, Volume 92 Number 6, September 1999.

Gullbery, John, *Mathematics from the Birth of Numbers*, © 1997, WW Norton and Co., 039304002X.

Johnson, David W., and Roger T. Johnson, *Meaningful Assessment: A Manageable and Cooperative Process*, © 2002, Allyn & Bacon, 0-205-32762-1.

Karush, William, *Webster's New World Dictionary of Mathematics*, Revised Edition, © 1989, MacMillan General Reference, 0131926675.

McKeachie, Wilber J., and Barbara K. Hofer, <u>*McKeachie's Teaching Tips: Strategies, Research, and Theory for College and University Teachers*</u>, © 2001, Houghton Mifflin Company, 0618116494.

Math Spanish Glossary, 2nd ed., © 2001, Addison-Wesley, 0-201-72896-6.

Royse, David, *Teaching Tips for College and University Instructors: A Practical Guide*, © 2000, Allyn & Bacon, 0205298397.

Web Links

http://mtsu32.mtsu.edu:11064/skill.html — Math study skills inventory

http://www.ltcconline.net/greenl/java/index.html#Intermediate%20and%20College%20Algebra — Interactive algebra lessons

http://www.prenhall.com/divisions/esm/app/calculator/medialib/ReferenceCenter/framesets/TechFeat83.html — A TI calculator site

http://mtsu32.mtsu.edu:11064/anxiety.html — Help with math anxiety

http://www.shodor.org/interactivate/activities/slopeslider/index.html — Applet for investigating lines and slope

http://occawlonline.pearsoned.com/bookbind/pubbooks/bittinger10_awl/ — The online resource for the textbook

www.awl.com/tutorcenter — Pearson Tutor Services

www.gomath.com — Online math help

www.freemathhelp.com/math-tutoring.html — Free math help (Algebra, Geometry, Calculus, Trig)

http://www.coolmath.com/graphit — Cool Math is a nice online graphing utility available at this site.

www.analyzemath.com — Analyze Math is an interactive mathematics site that provides applets to help students understand mathematical concepts.

http://math.exeter.edu/rparris — WinPlot is a freely distributed algebraic graphing program with a wide range of capabilities.

www.algebrahelp.com — Math help using technology

www.ictcm.org — International Conference on Technology in Collegiate Mathematics

www.maa.org — Mathematics Association of America

www.math.com — Resource for help with math homework

http://www.msubillings.edu/asc/graphing_calculators.htm — Directions for graphing calculators

http://www.univie.ac.at/future.media/moe/galerie/fun2/fun2.html — A gallery of multimedia learning materials — functions